# Microsoft®
# Visua
# Programming Projects
# ACTIVITIES WORKBOOK

## CEP, Inc.

## John Sestak

VISIT US ON THE INTERNET
# www.swep.com

South-Western Educational Publishing
*an International Thomson Publishing company* I(T)P®
www.thomson.com

Cincinnati • Albany, NY • Belmont, CA • Bonn • Boston • Detroit • Johannesburg • London • Madrid
Melbourne • Mexico City • New York • Paris • Singapore • Tokyo • Toronto • Washington

**Library of Congress Cataloging-in-Publication Data**

Sestak, John.

    Microsoft Visual Basic programming projects / John Sestak.

       p.   cm.

    ISBN 0-538-68894-7

    1.  Microsoft Visual BASIC.   2.  BASIC (Computer program language).

  I.  Title.

  QA76.73.B3S425   2000

  005.26'8—dc21                                             99-24245

                                                          CIP

| | |
|---|---|
| Managing Editor: | Carol Volz |
| Production Manager: | Dave Lafferty |
| Consulting Editor: | Custom Editorial Productions, Inc. |
| Marketing Manager: | Larry Qualls |
| Design Coordinator: | Mike Broussard |
| Production: | Custom Editorial Productions, Inc. |

Copyright © 2000

By SOUTH-WESTERN EDUCATIONAL PUBLISHING

Cincinnati, Ohio

ISBN: 0-538-68894-7

2  3  4  5  WE  02  01  00

Printed in the United States of America

I(T)P®

International Thomson Publishing

South-Western Educational Publishing is a division of International Thomson Publishing, Inc. The ITP registered trademark is used under license.

# PREFACE

The purpose of this project book is to reinforce the topics that you have been exposed to in your Visual Basic class. It supports the textbook from which you have been learning theory and will take you beyond the text into fun and enjoyable areas. The projects in this book should run on either the VB 5 or VB 6 compiler. No specific code sequences are designed to run on a specific compiler. However, if you create a project in VB 6, you will need to remove one line of code from the project file in order to run the project in VB 5. Open your VB 6 project file in Notepad, remove the line that reads "Retained = 0," and then save the file. Your VB 6 project will now run in VB 5.

## Using This Book

Each project and end-of-lesson application in this book is identified as either a beginner-(B), intermediate-(I), or advanced-(A) level activity. You will also notice that some exercises are marked with a SCANS icon. SCANS stands for the Secretary's Commission on Achieving Necessary Skills. A SCANS icon next to an exercise indicates that it satisfies a majority of the workplace competency and foundation skills identified by the commission.

This book is accompanied by the *Electronic Instructor* CD, which contains all the project files that you are instructed to create, answers to project and end-of-lesson review questions, and other components designed to enhance the learning experience.

## Acknowledgments

I would like to thank God for providing me with the ability to share my knowledge with others. I would also like to thank Todd Knowlton, Dr. Vladimir Uskov at the University of Cincinnati for his insightful review of the manuscript, and Tom Bockerstette for his thorough technical review. I would like to thank Betsy Newberry, Laura Citro, and the rest of the staff at Custom Editorial Productions, Inc., and South-Western Educational Publishing for their belief in my ability to create this book. And I would like to thank Walt Roncevic and Tom Roncevic, fellow instructors, for insights about what would prove useful to the students.

Last, but certainly not least, I would like to thank my wife, Trish, and our three rugrats, Ryan, Kristi, and Tim, for working with and around me as this book developed. I would also like to thank my mom and dad for their continued interest in my achievements. You realize that accomplishments become more meaningful when you have family that you can share them with.

John Sestak
Microsoft Certified Professional
Professional Trainer & Consultant
jsestak@pathway.net

# How to Use this Text

What makes a good computer programming text? Sound pedagogy and the most current, complete materials. That is what you will find in the new *Microsoft Visual Basic Programming Projects*. Not only will you find an inviting layout, but also many features to enhance learning.

**Objectives**— Objectives are listed at the beginning of each lesson, along with a suggested time for completion of the lesson. This allows you to look ahead to what you will be learning and to pace your work.

**Program Code Examples**—Many examples of program code are included in the text to illustrate concepts under discussion.

**Projects**—Projects present hands on application of programming concepts and show the analysis, design, and implementation stages of the software development life cycle.

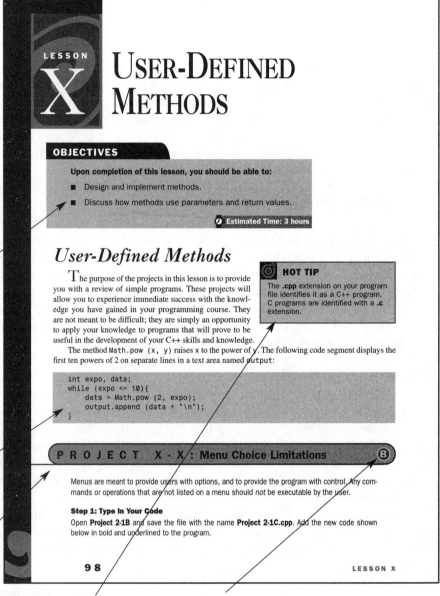

**LESSON X**

# USER-DEFINED METHODS

### OBJECTIVES

**Upon completion of this lesson, you should be able to:**

■ Design and implement methods.

■ Discuss how methods use parameters and return values.

*Estimated Time: 3 hours*

## User-Defined Methods

The purpose of the projects in this lesson is to provide you with a review of simple programs. These projects will allow you to experience immediate success with the knowledge you have gained in your programming course. They are not meant to be difficult; they are simply an opportunity to apply your knowledge to programs that will prove to be useful in the development of your C++ skills and knowledge.

The method Math.pow (x, y) raises x to the power of y. The following code segment displays the first ten powers of 2 on separate lines in a text area named output:

```
int expo, data;
while (expo <= 10){
    data = Math.pow (2, expo);
    output.append (data + "\n");
}
```

**HOT TIP**

The **.cpp** extension on your program file identifies it as a C++ program. C programs are identified with a **.c** extension.

### PROJECT X - X: Menu Choice Limitations

Menus are meant to provide users with options, and to provide the program with control. Any commands or operations that are not listed on a menu should *not* be executable by the user.

**Step 1: Type In Your Code**
Open **Project 2-1B** and save the file with the name **Project 2-1C.cpp**. Add the new code shown below in bold and underlined to the program.

**98**    LESSON X

**Hot Tip**—These boxes provide enrichment information about Visual Basic.

**Skill Level Icons**— Each project and end-of-lesson activity is identified as either a beginner (B), intermediate (I), or advanced (A) level exercise.

**Concept Builder—** These boxes provide additional, important information about the features being discussed.

**Summary—**At the end of each lesson, you will find a summary to help you complete the end-of-lesson activities.

**Review Questions—** Review material at the end of each lesson and each unit enables you to prepare for assessment of the content presented.

**SCANS** (Secretary's Commission on Achieving Necessary Skills)—The U.S. Department of Labor has identified the school-to-careers competencies. The five workplace competencies (resources, interpersonal skills, information, systems, and technology) and foundation skills (basic skills, thinking skills, and personal qualities) are identified in Projects and end-of-lesson activities throughout the text. More information on SCANS can be found on the *Electronic Instructor.*

---

**Step 2: Add Your Code to the Event**

If you were to "run" this program right now, you would have a decent-looking form that opened, accepted text into the "Enter Miles" box, and then did nothing—unless you maximized, minimized, or closed the form. VB is *event* driven

> **CONCEPT BUILDER**
>
> Do not limit yourself to VB in designing programs. Notice how all GUI applications interact with their users.

*Lesson X User-Defined Methods*

## *Summary*

In this lesson, you learned:

- The modern computer age began in the late 1940s with the development of ENIAC. Business computing became practical in the 1950s, and time-sharing computers advanced computing in large organizations in the 1960s.

### LESSON X REVIEW QUESTIONS

#### WRITTEN QUESTIONS

**Write your answers to the following questions.**

1. What are the three major hardware components of a computer?
2. Name three input devices.

### TESTING YOUR SKILLS

#### APPLICATION X-X

> **Estimated Time:**
> Application 1-1  30 minutes
> Application 1-2  30 minutes
> Application 1-3  30 minutes

1. Add code to Project 1-1 that converts kilometers into miles.
   a. Open the **Project 1-1** program file.
   b. After the code that creates the output of the miles to kilometers conversion, add the necessary lines to perform a kilometers to miles conversion. The lines of code should be similar to the code used for the original program.

   *HINT:* The conversion this time is going in reverse. Use your algebra skills!

   c. Save your revised program as **App1-1.**

### CRITICAL THINKING

> **Estimated Time: 1 hour**

You have an idea for a program that will help the local pizza shop handle take-out orders. Your friend suggests an interview with the shop's owner to discuss her user requirements before you get started on the program. Explain why this is a good suggestion, and list the questions you would ask the owner to help you determine the user requirements.

**99**

---

**Testing Your Skills—** End-of-lesson hands-on application of what has been learned in the lesson allows you to actually apply the techniques covered.

**Critical Thinking Activity—**Each lesson gives you an opportunity to apply creative analysis to situations presented.

# CONTENTS

# Try These Projects for More Programming Practice

## Exciting new products from South-Western!

Our new Visual Basic and C++ programming activities workbooks offer additional projects that reinforce introductory instruction on these programming languages. These cover everything from beginning, to intermediate, to advanced topics to meet your programming needs.

- **NEW!** *Microsoft® Visual Basic Programming Projects, Activities Workbook* (CEP, Inc. & Sestak)
  Has 10 lessons with 32 projects. Also, there are 18 applications exercises and 10 critical thinking projects. These projects number over 35 hours of instruction on the most widely used beginning through advanced features of Visual Basic.
  | | |
  |---|---|
  | Text, soft cover, 240 pages | 0-538-68894-7 |
  | Electronic Instructor CD-ROM Package, 96 pages | 0-538-68895-5 |

## Other Complementary Texts:

- **Using Visual Basic, Second Edition** (Sprague) Covers computer science fundamentals using Visual Basic and is appropriate for a variety of courses with over 35+ hours of instruction. Covers versions 2-5.
  | | |
  |---|---|
  | Text, hard cover, 672 pages | 0-538-67886-0 |
  | Workbook, 224 pages | 0-538-67887-9 |
  | Instructor's Manual/Solutions Disk Package, 256 pages | 0-538-67893-3 |
  | Testing Software | 0-538-65187-3 |

- **NEW!** *Microsoft® Visual Basic 6.0 Basics* (Knowlton and Collings) A short course introductory book with over 20+ hours of instruction.
  | | |
  |---|---|
  | Text/Data Disk Package, soft cover, 320 pages | 0-538-69086-0 |
  | Workbook, 128 pages | 0-538-69084-4 |
  | Electronic Instructor CD-ROM Package, 112 pages | 0-538-69085-2 |
  | Testing Software | 0-538-to come |

- **NEW!** *Microsoft® Visual Basic 6.0 Introduction to Programming* (Sprague & Phillips)
  Is a comprehensive text with over 35+ hours of instruction. MCSD-certified!
  | | |
  |---|---|
  | Text, hard cover, 608 pages | 0-538-68818-1 |
  | Text/Data CD-ROM Package, soft cover | 0-538-68816-5 |
  | Workbook/Data CD-ROM Package, 160 pages | 0-538-68915-3 |
  | MCSD Certification Workbook,/Data CD-ROM Package, 320 pages | 0-538-69137-9 |
  | Electronic Instructor CD-ROM Package, 128 pages | 0-538-68820-3 |
  | Testing Software | 0-538-to come |

- **ALSO NEW!** *C++ Programming Projects, Activities Workbook* (CEP, Inc. & Sestak)
  Has over 10 lessons with 50 projects. Also, there are 30 applications exercises and 11 critical thinking projects. These projects number over 35 hours of instruction on the most widely used beginning through advanced features of C++.
  | | |
  |---|---|
  | Text, soft cover, 272 pages | 0-538-69081-X |
  | Electronic Instructor CD-ROM Package, 96 pages | 0-538-69082-8 |

A new feature available for these products is the Electronic Instructor, which includes a printed Instructor's manual and a CD-ROM. The CD-ROM contains tests, lesson plans, all solutions files, and more! Also, ask about our ProgramPaks for compiler software bundles!

**Join Us On the Internet**
**www.swep.com**

South-Western
Educational Publishing

# *List of Projects*

# SIMPLE PROGRAMS

## OBJECTIVES

**Upon completion of this lesson, you should be able to:**

■ Describe the Visual Basic environment.

■ Explain the process of program development.

■ Demonstrate your understanding of Visual Basic.

■ Produce working applications from the instructions provided.

■ Practice the concepts learned in your programming course.

 **Estimated Time: 4 hours**

## *Introduction*

$T$he purpose of the projects in this lesson is to provide you with a review of the more common *controls* used in Visual Basic. These projects will allow you to experience immediate success with the knowledge you have gained in your programming course. The projects in this lesson are not meant to be difficult; rather, they are meant to be fun and useful. They are simply a first step on your journey through the Visual Basic programming language.

Visual Basic (VB) is both a language and an *application development tool,* although the information technology industry generally categorizes VB as just an application development tool. Regardless of which view you take, it is very popular, very useful, and intuitive and very much in demand. As you may have noticed, VB approaches programming from a "backward" point of view. Instead of planning the flow or execution of the program and then writing the code as you would in *structured programming,* you now plan the layout and then write the code! This has caused torment for many programmers who are not used to thinking in this manner. However, this way of programming is much more efficient for a variety of reasons. One is that the programmer can build *user-friendliness* into the program from the start.

Even though program development seems to be reversed in VB, this does not remove the need for good programming technique. Good code is still structured; however, it is now attached to a control and is triggered by an *event* instead of executing in a *sequence*. The sequence is now in the hands of the user, who gets to decide when things happen.

This lesson will focus on the following:

■ **Describing the Visual Basic environment.** You will review the Visual Basic environment. Visual Basic 6.0 is the compiler used to create projects for this book; however, the differences between 6.0 and earlier versions are minimal.

■ **Explaining the process of program development.** You will learn about program development as it relates to Visual Basic. Remember that you begin by designing the interface and then move into coding the execution of the program with VB. This has caused concern with some programmers, so we will attempt to eliminate those concerns immediately.

■ **Demonstrating your understanding of Visual Basic.** You will be required to use the skills and abilities that you have acquired through your Visual Basic course. This book explains and reinforces important topics; however, the basics are your responsibility.

■ **Producing working applications from the instructions provided.** Every project will end with a working form or application that may require enhancement but should work.

■ **Practicing the concepts learned in your programming course.** Everything you do in this projects book will reinforce the topics covered in your programming course. This book also attempts to take you beyond the basics with Critical Thinking exercises at the end of each lesson.

## PROJECT 1-1 : Miles to Kilometers Conversion  Ⓑ

This project begins with a quick overview of the VB 6.0 environment. You will explore the parts of the *interface*, and then develop your first program, which will convert miles to kilometers. It will use some of the more common VB controls, such as *labels*, *text boxes*, and *command buttons*. You will also manipulate some of the **properties** of each control. Remember that everything in VB has properties, including the form itself.

### Step 1: Start Your Compiler

The programs in this book have been developed with Microsoft Visual Basic 6.0. This compiler can be used stand-alone or in conjunction with Microsoft's Visual Studio 6. The figures in this book were generated in the VB 6.0 environment. The programs you develop, however, will run on previous versions of VB. If there are differences, they will be noted.

Start your compiler.

Figure 1-1 shows the VB development interface, which you should be familiar with from your VB programming course. However, a quick overview will refresh your understanding of the terminology.

**FIGURE 1-1**
VB development interface

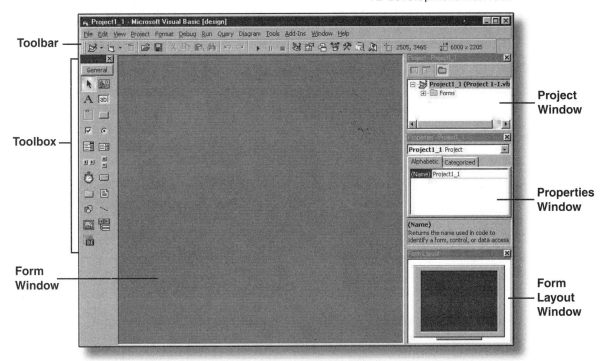

Students of VB often confuse the toolbar with the toolbox. The **_toolbar_** is the "bar" that normally stretches across the top of the Visual Basic window. It contains the Open, Save, Cut, Paste, and other buttons used for VB projects. The **_toolbox_** is the "strip" of tools that is generally positioned vertically on the left side of the VB window. It contains the controls that you place on forms. Make sure you understand the difference between the two.

The other parts of the environment are the Form window editing area, the Project window, the Properties window, and the Form Layout window. The Form window editing area is where you perform your layout work.

The Project window lists all the components that belong to a project in a treelike listing. The Properties window displays all the properties that belong to whichever control is highlighted. The Form Layout window displays the location where your forms will display on the screen when your program is executed.

Now that you know which component is which, let's get to work!

### Step 2: Create a New Project

Click **File** on the Menu bar. When the drop-down menu appears, click **New Project**. In the New Project window, double-click the **Standard EXE** button. Your VB environment should look like Figure 1-2.

The Project1 window displays with a blank form, Form1, opened.

**FIGURE 1-2**
Creating a new project

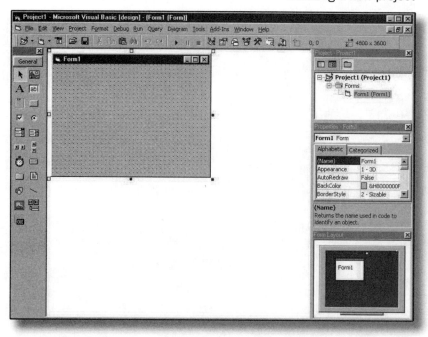

## Step 3: Add Your Controls

Before adding controls, the first thing you should do is to resize your form to the size you think it should be. Keep in mind that this new size is not going to be "carved in stone." If you need to change the size again, and you probably will, you can change it very easily. Resize your form so that it looks like Figure 1-3.

**FIGURE 1-3**
Resizing the form

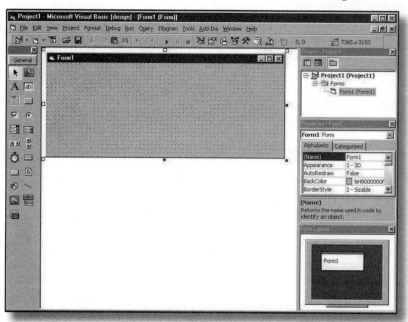

Now let's place our controls. Place two label controls, two text box controls, and one command button on the form, as shown in Figure 1-4. Size each control and the form to the approximate size of those shown in the figure.

**HOT TIP**

The text boxes used for numbers should be just tall enough to hold the numbers. This adds to the aesthetics of the form.

**FIGURE 1-4**
Placing controls on a form

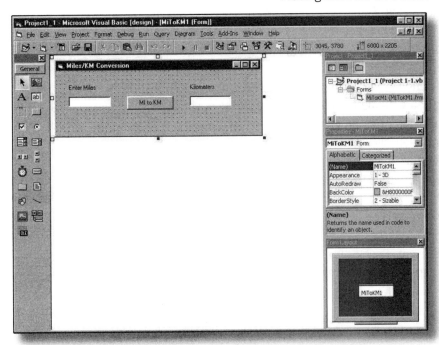

Position the form in the middle of the Form Layout window. Change the appropriate properties for each control, as outlined in the following chart:

| Control | Name | Caption |
|---|---|---|
| Project | Project1_1 | No caption |
| Form | MiToKM1 | Miles/KM Conversion |
| Text1 | txtMiles | No caption, no text |
| Text2 | txtConvKM | No caption, no text |
| Label1 | lblMiles | Enter Miles |
| Label2 | lblKMAnswer | Kilometers |
| Command1 | _____ | MI to KM |

**Step 4: Save Your Project**

Click **File** on the Menu bar. When the drop-down menu appears, click **Save Project As**. In the Save File As dialog box, select the proper folder assigned to you by your teacher in which to save project files, then change the default file name to **MiToKM1**, which is the same name given to the form. This is a good way to ensure consistency. Then click the **Save** button.

Once the form file is saved, the Save Project As dialog box opens. Make sure you are in the same folder that your teacher assigned to you. Then rename the project to **Project 1-1**. Click the **Save** button. Once the project is saved, the information displayed in the Project window should look the same as in Figure 1-4.

Remember, it is always a good idea to save your projects *often*. Do not wait until you are near completion because it is very easy to lose all your hard work!

### Step 5: Add Your Code to the Event

If you were to "run" this program right now, you would have a decent-looking form that opened, accepted text into the "Enter Miles" box, and then did nothing—unless you maximized, minimized, or closed the form. VB is *event* driven, which means that users need to decide what they want to happen; then they need to *trigger* the event. Just as a gun's trigger is pulled to fire a bullet, in VB you perform an action, and then an event occurs. In this case, the trigger is a click on the command button.

When you click the MI to KM command button, you would expect the miles entered to be converted to kilometers and then displayed in the Kilometers text box. In order for that to happen, you need to code the event. This is where VB is quite different from structured programming.

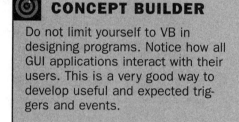

**CONCEPT BUILDER**

Do not limit yourself to VB in designing programs. Notice how all GUI applications interact with their users. This is a very good way to develop useful and expected triggers and events.

Instead of adding code the way you do in a sequence-structured environment, you add it to the control that will trigger the event. Double-click the **MI to KM** command button. The Form window editing area opens to display the code attached to the command button, as shown in Figure 1-5.

**FIGURE 1-5**
Code attached to command button

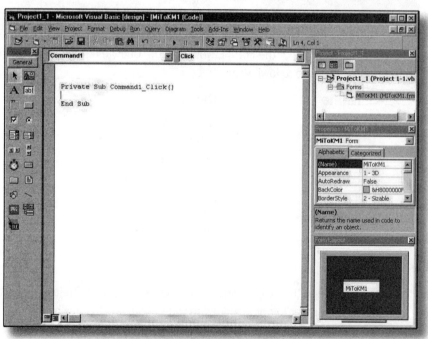

It is now up to you to add the appropriate code. So enter the following line of code on the blank line between the two lines of attached code.

```
txtConvKM.Text = txtMiles / 0.62
```

Then make sure you save both the form and the project again. Simply clicking the **Save** button on the toolbar will save the entire project. We are now ready to run our program for the first time.

### Step 6: Run the Program

VB offers both an *interpreted* version and a *compiled* version built into the same compiler. When you first run and test a program, it will be interpreted, not compiled. The difference is that an interpreted program is run as you write it, whereas a compiled program is actually turned into machine code and is no longer in the language in which it was written.

The beauty of this "interpretation" is that it makes *debugging* much easier. You can remove all the bugs and then compile the program so that it cannot be easily modified.

To run your program, simply click the **Run** button on the toolbar. Your program should open in the middle of the screen. If you input a number of miles and click on the command button, your program should convert the miles to kilometers and display the conversion in the Kilometers text box. Let's do an easy test: Key in **6.2** miles. The conversion will give you 10 kilometers.

### Step 7: Review Your Code

Now that your program has run successfully, answer the following questions. Review your answers with your classmates and teacher.

**1.** Why do the control names begin with lowercase, three-letter prefixes, such as lbl and txt?

_____

_____

_____

**2.** In Step 3, the name of the command button was intentionally left blank. The name VB gave to the button is Command1. Provide a better name for the command button using the correct three-letter prefix.

_____

**3.** Explain the difference between the Name and Caption properties.

_____

_____

**4.** Explain the following line of code.

```
txtConvKM.Text = txtMiles / 0.62
```

_____

_____

**5.** Explain the specific event that triggers this program to work.

_____

**7**

**6.** Explain the difference between a label and a text box.

_____

_____

_____

**7.** Explain the difference between the form and project names as they appear in their properties list, and the filenames given to them when saved.

_____

_____

_____

**8.** Explain the overall execution of the program.

_____

_____

_____

_____

You now have a working Visual Basic program! Before you move on to the next project, let's look at one more detail.

### Step 8: Create an Executable Program

Create an executable file that you can transport from computer to computer.

Open the File menu and click **Make Project 1-1.exe**. The Make Project dialog box opens, prompting you for a folder in which to save your .exe file. Save your .exe file in the same folder assigned to you by your teacher. Name your project **Miles To KM Conversion** and then click the **Save** button. The window will close, and in the upper left corner of your VB window, you will notice that VB tells you that it is compiling and then creating the executable file. When it is finished, you will find the executable file in your personal folder.

Just for fun, move the executable program to your desktop and run it, or copy it to a floppy and take it home to run on your own PC. You now have a program that runs and an executable version that you can take with you. You can do this with any program you write in VB! The fun is just beginning!

## P R O J E C T   1 - 2 : Bank Balance Calculation   Ⓑ

Now that you have one project under your belt, let's create another simple project. This time you will use labels, text boxes, and a command button again, but you will add some enhancements to both code and the control properties.

You will be duplicating a bank reconciliation calculation. The user will input the information requested using multiple text boxes and labels. When the information is input, a click on the command button will cause the calculation to be performed. This is a simple but effective program.

### Step 1: Start Your Compiler

Start your compiler if it is not already running.

### Step 2: Create a New Project

Open the **File** menu and click **New Project**. In the New Project dialog box, double-click the **Standard EXE** button. Your VB environment should be ready for you to begin work.

### Step 3: Add Your Controls

Resize your form so that it looks like Figure 1-6. Notice that the project and form are numbered 1 by default. You will be changing the names, captions, and other properties later in this project.

**FIGURE 1-6**
Resizing a form

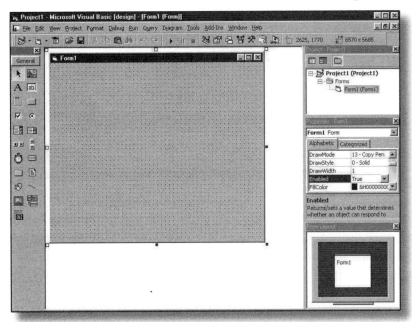

Now let's place the controls. Place five label controls, five text box controls, and one command button on the form as shown in Figure 1-7. Size the controls so that they are the approximate size of those shown in the figure. Position the form in the middle of the Form Layout window. Change the appropriate properties for each control as outlined in the following chart:

| Control | Name | Caption |
|---|---|---|
| Project | Project1_2 | No caption |
| Form | BankBal | Bank Balance Calculation |
| Text1 | txtBankBal | No caption, no text |
| Text2 | txtOutDep | No caption, no text |
| Text3 | txtSubtotal | No caption, no text |
| Text4 | txtOutChecks | No caption, no text |
| Text5 | txtAdjBank | No caption, no text |
| Label1 | lblBankBal | Bank Balance |
| Label2 | lblOutDep | Outstanding Deposits |
| Label3 | lblSubtotal | Subtotal |
| Label4 | lblOutChecks | Outstanding Checks |
| Label5 | lblAdjBank | Adjusted Bank Balance |
| Command1 | cmdCalculate | Calculate |

**FIGURE 1-7**
Placing controls

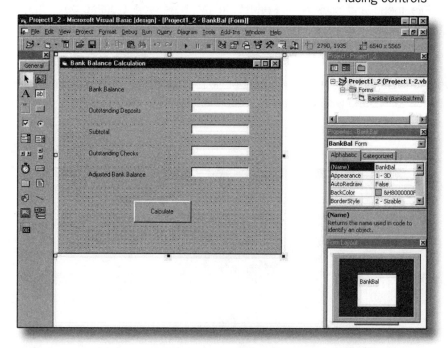

One additional property that will be changed for this program is the Enabled property for the txtSubtotal and the txtAdjBank text boxes. Click on the **txtSubtotal** text box and scroll down the properties list until you find the **Enabled** property. Double-click the **True** value to change it to **False**. Perform the same steps on the **textAdjBank** object. This will prevent the user from entering text into these two boxes. You want them to input text in each text box, except for these two, because these will display the results of your calculations.

### Step 4: Save Your Project

Open the File menu and click **Save Project As**. In the Save File As dialog box, select the proper folder assigned to you by your teacher, then change the default file name to **BankBal**, which is the same name given to the form. Click the **Save** button.

Once the form file is saved, the Save Project As dialog box opens. Make sure you are in the same folder that your teacher assigned to you. Then rename the project to **Project 1-2**. Click the **Save** button. Once the project is saved, the information displayed in the Project window should look the same as in Figure 1-7.

Remember to save your projects *often*.

### Step 5: Add Your Code to the Event

Add code to the control that will trigger the event. Double-click the **Calculate** command button. The Form window editing area opens to display the code attached to the command button, as shown in Figure 1-8.

**FIGURE 1-8**

Code attached to Calculate command button

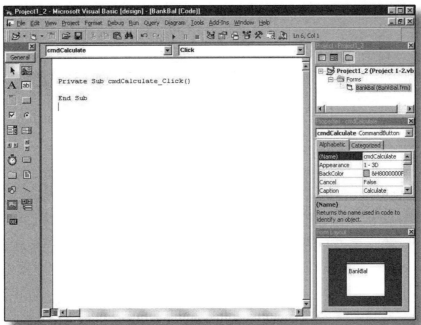

Enter the following lines of code on the blank line between the command button code:

```
txtSubtotal.Text = Val(txtBankBal.Text) + Val(txtOutDep.Text)
txtAdjBank.Text = Val(txtSubtotal.Text) - Val(txtOutChecks.Text)
```

Then make sure you save both the form and the project again. Simply click the **Save** button on the toolbar. You are now ready to run the program for the first time.

**Step 6: Run the Program**

To run your program, simply click the **Run** button on the toolbar. Your program should open in the middle of the screen. If you input a bank balance, the amount of outstanding deposits, and the amount of outstanding checks, and then click on the command button, your program should calculate the subtotal and the adjusted bank balance. Test the program by inputting amounts into each of those three text boxes.

**Step 7: Review Your Code**

Now that your program has run successfully, answer the following questions. Review your answers with your classmates and teacher.

1. Why do the control names begin with lowercase, three-letter prefixes, such as lbl, txt, and cmd?

_____

_____

_____

**2.** Explain the Enabled text box property.

_____

_____

_____

**3.** What happens to the text displayed in the text boxes where the Enabled property is set to False?

_____

_____

_____

**4.** Explain the following lines of code.

```
txtSubtotal.Text = Val(txtBankBal.Text) + Val(txtOutDep.Text)
txtAdjBank.Text = Val(txtSubtotal.Text) - Val(txtOutChecks.Text)
```

_____

_____

_____

_____

_____

**5.** What would happen if the Val() were not used?

_____

_____

_____

**6.** Explain the specific event that triggers this program to work.

_____

_____

**7.** Explain the difference between a label and a text box.

_____

_____

_____

**8.** Explain the difference between the form and project names as they appear in their properties list, and the filenames given to them when saved.

_____

_____

_____

**9.** Explain the overall execution of the program.

_____

_____

_____

_____

_____

You now have another working Visual Basic program. If you would like, you can create an executable version of your program the same way you did with Project 1-1. The process is no different. If you are not sure of the process, review Step 8 of Project 1-1.

# Summary

This lesson provided a quick review of the Visual Basic programming environment. You created a program that performed a miles-to-kilometer conversion that consisted of one form, two labels, two text boxes, and one command button. When the user input a number of miles in the Enter Miles text box and then clicked on the command button, the program converted the miles into kilometers and displayed the answer in the Kilometers text box.

The second program you created was slightly more complex. It performed a simple financial calculation and included five labels and five text boxes. You also enhanced the Subtotal and the Adjust Bank Balance text boxes so that the user could not input data to these. The output of these text boxes was also slightly different from the others.

## LESSON 1 REVIEW QUESTIONS

### SHORT ANSWER

**Define the following in the space provided.**

**1.** Visual Basic

_____

_____

_____

**2.** Controls

_____

_____

**3.** Application development tool

_____

_____

_____

**4.** Structured programming

_____

_____

_____

_____

**5.** User-friendly

_____

_____

_____

_____

**6.** Trigger

_____

_____

**7.** Event

_____

_____

**8.** Sequence

_____

_____

_____

**9.** Interface

_____

_____

**10.** Label

_____

_____

_____

11. Text box

_____

12. Command button

_____

_____

_____

13. Properties

_____

_____

_____

14. Toolbar

_____

_____

15. Toolbox

_____

_____

16. Name

_____

_____

17. Caption

_____

_____

18. Interpreted

_____

_____

_____

19. Compiled

_____

_____

_____

_____

**20.** .exe file

_____

_____

_____

**21.** Debug

_____

_____

## WRITTEN QUESTIONS

**Write your answers to the following questions in the space provided.**

1.  Explain why Visual Basic is considered an application development tool by the information technology industry.

    _____

    _____

    _____

2.  Explain how Visual Basic is both an interpreted and a compiled language.

    _____

    _____

    _____

3.  Explain the difference between toolbar and toolbox.

    _____

    _____

    _____

4.  Explain the relationship between triggers and events.

    _____

    _____

5.  Explain the difference between a structured programming language and an event-driven language.

    _____

    _____

    _____

    _____

    _____

## TESTING YOUR SKILLS

Estimated Time:

Application 1-1  1 hour
Application 1-2  1 hour
Application 1-3  1 hour

### APPLICATION 1-1  B

1. Modify Project 1-1 so that an additional conversion takes place—converting kilometers to miles. Save your modified project as **App1-1**.

2. Add two additional text boxes and one additional command button.

3. Add the code needed for the additional command button.

### APPLICATION 1-2  I

1. Draw, label, and explain the six major parts of the Visual Basic environment.

### APPLICATION 1-3  I

This application will expand upon Project 1-1. Your form will contain three controls—two text boxes and one command button. The layout will be similar to Project 1-1. The user will input text in the first text box. This text will appear in one font style. When the user clicks the command button, the text from the first text box will appear in the second text box—with one modification: The font style will be different.

The font styles are your choice. A neat possibility is to have one box display symbols. This gives you a "code" in which to write notes to your friends. Your program will serve as the "translator." Remember: You can create an executable file that everyone can put on their own PC.

Save this program as **App1-3**.

## CRITICAL THINKING  A

Estimated Time: 2 hours

Create a program (similar to Project 1-1), that converts Fahrenheit temperature to the Celsius scale and back again.

# USER INTERACTION

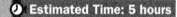

## OBJECTIVES

**Upon completion of this lesson, you should be able to:**

■ Define user interaction.

■ Explain the reasons for user interaction.

■ Design interfaces for user interaction.

■ Integrate additional controls.

■ Modify additional control properties.

**⏱ Estimated Time: 5 hours**

## *Introduction*

U*ser interaction* means allowing the user to control various aspects of the program. Computer programs are written for an individual or a group of individuals. Knowing who the user is and what he or she needs from the program is a very important part of *program design*. You, as the programmer, need to identify the *end users* and gather information from them. The information you gather provides you with valuable insight about both the execution of the program and the development of the *program interface*.

Visual Basic is by default a user-oriented development tool. You begin by designing the form, or interface, and then you build in the *functionality*. This method of programming lends itself to making programs *user friendly*. By providing the user with an interface that is logical (the user can easily determine what should be done) and that controls the actions of the user (limited by command buttons), you can make your program user friendly but at the same time maintain control over the execution.

Visual Basic provides the programmer with a variety of *controls*, each of which possesses a variety of *properties*. In Lesson 1 you were introduced to a few of the more commonly used controls. In this lesson you become familiar with additional controls that lend themselves to the development of interfaces. You will create controls that allow the user to "take control" of the program. This can be accomplished simply by providing text boxes for input and then limiting the command button options available to the user. As you will see, user interaction is a very important part of program development.

This lesson focuses on the following:

■ **Defining user interaction.** You will learn to define various ways that the user can interact with your programs by creating forms that prompt the user for action.

■ **Explaining the reasons for user interaction.** You will be able to share your knowledge with other programmers regarding proper methods of user interaction. Each form you design and each project you complete will increase your abilities.

■ **Designing interfaces for user interaction.** You will design various interfaces for the projects in this lesson that will provide you with a basic understanding of user interaction. From this basic understanding you will able to expand your abilities into more sophisticated techniques.

■ **Integrating additional controls.** Each lesson provides you with an understanding of additional controls, which will be shown in a manner that is particular to the projects you are creating; however, the use of the controls can also be applied in other areas.

■ **Modifying additional control properties.** As you learn about additional controls, you will also be presented with the use of some of their properties. It will be almost impossible to present you with a working knowledge of every property of every control; however, you will gain the confidence to experiment with some of the unmentioned controls on your own.

## PROJECT 2 - 1 : Simple Menu (B)

Many programs begin with menu forms that allow users to choose the activities they would like to perform. You will usually see menu forms in programs that do more than one thing. There was no need to use a menu form with the miles-to-kilometers program in Lesson 1 because the program was simple and self-explanatory. However, if you were to provide access to a *database* that allowed users a variety of options, then you would want to exercise some control by providing the users with a list of choices.

In this project, you will create a simple menu containing five choice options. Selecting a choice will trigger a specific event. This lets the user choose what he or she would like to do while allowing you to maintain control over your program. This interface will not be totally functional because some of the needed components are not introduced until later lessons. However, it will work to the point that you will be able to understand the functionality of the choices.

### Step 1: Start Your Compiler

If it is not already running, start your compiler.

### Step 2: Create a New Project

Open the **File** menu, and click **New Project**. In the New Project dialog box, double-click the **Standard EXE** button. Your VB environment should look like Figure 2-1.

The Project1 file opens, displaying a blank form named Form1.

Starting a new project

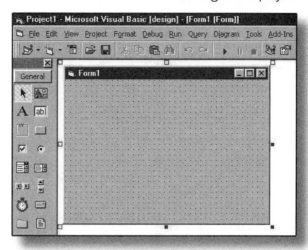

## Step 3: Add Your Controls

Resize your form so that it looks like Figure 2-2. You will notice that the project and form are numbered 1 by default. You will change the names, captions, and other properties later.

**FIGURE 2-2**
Changing the size of the form

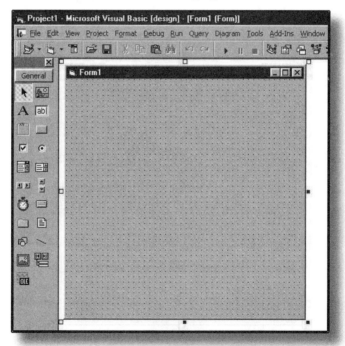

Remember that you can always change the size of the form again later.

Now let's place your controls. Place five label controls, five command buttons, and one text box control as shown in Figure 2-3. Size each control and the form so that they are the approximate size of those shown in the figure. (*Hint:* The text boxes used for text should be just tall enough to hold the text. This adds to the aesthetics of the form.) Position the form in the middle of the Form Layout window. Change the appropriate properties for each control as outlined in the following chart:

| Control | Name | Caption |
| --- | --- | --- |
| Project | Project2_1 | None |
| Form | frmSimpleMenu | Simple Menu |
| Label1 | lblAdd | Add A New Record |
| Label2 | lblModify | Modify An Existing Record |
| Label3 | lblDelete | Delete An Existing Record |
| Label4 | lblView | View/Print An Existing Record |
| Label5 | lblExit | Exit |
| Command1 | com1 | 1 |
| Command2 | com2 | 2 |
| Command3 | com3 | 3 |
| Command4 | com4 | 4 |
| Command5 | com5 | 5 |
| Text1 | txtResponse | No text (Caption is not a text box property) |

**FIGURE 2-3**
Placing controls

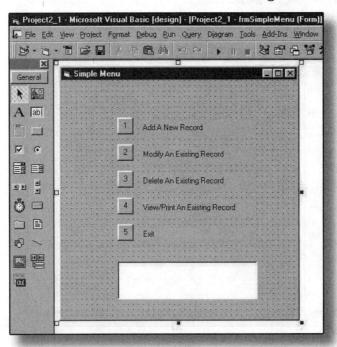

### Step 4: Save Your Project

Open the **File** menu and click **Save Project As**. In the Save File As dialog box, change the default filename to **SimpleMenu**, which is the same name given to the form. This is a good way to ensure consistency. Select the folder and/or disk containing your course files. Then click the **Save** button.

Once the form file is saved, the Save Project As dialog box opens. Make sure you are saving to the same course folder. Then rename the project to **Project 2-1**. Click the **Save** button. Once the project is saved, the information displayed in the Project window should look the same as in Figure 2-3.

Remember to save your projects often!

### Step 5: Add Your Code to the Event

As you have learned, VB is event driven, which means that users need to decide what they want to happen; then they need to trigger the event. The trigger is each command button.

When you click on any one of the command buttons, the appropriate action should be performed. In order for that to happen, you need to code the event.

Remember, you add the code to the control that will trigger the event. For this project, you will need to double-click each command button in order to enter the necessary code for each event. The Form window editing area will open to display the code attached to each command button. Figure 2-4 shows the code window that will open when you double-click the com1 button.

**FIGURE 2-4**
Command button code

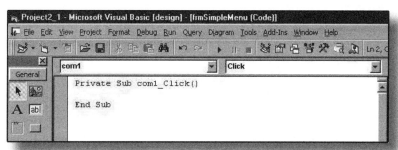

Enter the following line of code on the blank line between the lines of command button code:

```
txtResponse = "You chose to add a new record!"
```

Make sure you save both the form and the project again by clicking the **Save** button on the toolbar.

You now need to add code to the other command buttons. This is different from the coding you did in Lesson 1 in that you used only one or at most two command buttons. In this project you must code every command button that will be used to trigger an event! And every command button in this project will trigger an event.

Notice from the code added to com1 that another form will not open, at least not at this time. Multiple-form projects will be introduced later in this book, and the projects from this lesson will be modified to become completely functional at that time.

Now add the code necessary for the remaining four command buttons as shown in Figure 2-5.

**FIGURE 2-5**

Add code for four remaining command buttons

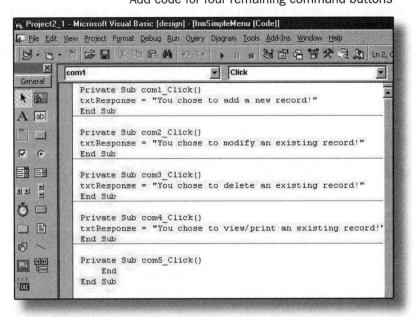

## Step 6: Run the Program

Click the **Run** button on the toolbar to run your program. Your program should open in the middle of the screen. If you click on any command button (with the exception of the Exit button), your program should display the purpose of the chosen command button in the text box. Click your way through the command buttons to make sure each one works properly, saving the Exit button for last. Click the **Exit** button to exit the program.

## Step 7: Review Your Code

Now that your program has run successfully, answer the following questions. Review your answers with your classmates and teacher.

**1.** The command buttons in this project are named com1 through com5. Is this the correct VB naming convention? Explain why or why not.

_____

_____

**2.** The line of code entered for each command button begins with txtResponse. Because your program executes, the lines of code work OK. However, is there a better syntax that should be used with the txtResponse? If so, write it in the following space.

_____

_____

**3.** Explain the purpose of a menu form.

_____

**4.** Explain the following line of code:

```
txtResponse = "You chose to add a new record!"
```

**5.** Explain the specific event that triggers any command button in this program to work.

**6.** Explain the following block of code:

```
Private Sub com5_Click()
    End
End Sub
```

**7.** Explain the overall execution of the program.

You now have a working simple menu program. Remember that the full functionality will be added in later lessons in this book. Next you will learn how to enhance your menu.

## PROJECT 2-2: Headings and Additional Control Properties

In this project you will add a label control that will serve as the heading for your simple menu.

You will insert the new label control at the top of the form and then change its *font* and *background color*. You will be instructed on the font and background color to apply, but feel free to change both to suit your own personal tastes.

One thing to keep in mind as you format controls is that end users expect some consistency. They expect fonts to look the same and to be readable, and they expect the colors to somehow relate to the program's purpose or to the "family" of programs to which it belongs. So, even though you will have complete control over color schemes and fonts, don't get too carried away!

### Step 1: Start Your Compiler

Start your compiler, if necessary.

### Step 2: Open Project 2-1

Open the **File** menu and click **Open Project**. In the Open Project dialog box, you have the choice of clicking the Existing or Recent tabs. If you choose the Existing tab, you can select the folder your project is in and then select the file to open. Once you have selected the file, click **Open**. If you select the Recent tab, you will see a list of recent projects you have worked with. If the file you want to open is on the list, select it, and click the **Open** button. For this project, open **Project 2-1**.

**2 5**

**Step 3: Add Your Controls**

Add a label control to your form that is the approximate size of the Record Menu heading shown in Figure 2-6. You will be changing the name, caption, and other properties of this label to make it look similar to the one shown in the figure.

**FIGURE 2-6**
Adding a label control

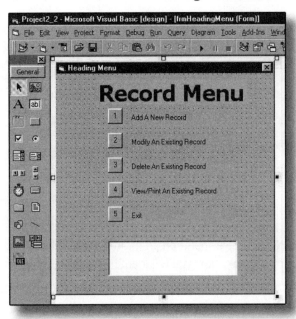

Change the properties of the label control as outlined in the following chart:

| Property | Value |
| --- | --- |
| Name | lblHeading |
| Caption | Record Menu |
| Font | Tahoma, Bold, 28 |
| BackColor | &H00FFFF00& |
| ForeColor | &H00800000& |

Now you will change the names of some of the other controls in order to make this project and form unique. Change the appropriate properties for other controls as outlined in the following chart:

| Control | Name | Caption |
| --- | --- | --- |
| Project | Project2_2 | None |
| Form | frmHeadingMenu | Heading Menu |

**Step 4: Save Your Project**

Open the **File** menu and click **Save File As**. Change the default file name to **HeadingMenu**, the same name given to the form. This is a good way to ensure consistency. Then, click the **Save** button.

Once the form file is saved, save the project. Open the **File** menu and click **Save Project As**. Save the project as **Project 2-2**. Then click the **Save** button. Your Project window should look similar to Figure 2-6.

### Step 5: Run Your Program

The program should run exactly as it did in Project 2-1. The only difference is that the menu form now displays a colorful heading label.

You now have an enhanced working Visual Basic program. If you would like, you can modify this program by changing fonts and color schemes. Remember that the user expects consistency, so do not go wild with your color selections.

## P R O J E C T   2 - 3 : Data Input Screen  (B)

Menus are the first step in creating the user interface. Now that users have a starting point, you need to continue leading them through your program. Each menu choice will lead to either another menu offering more specific choices or to a form that allows the user to interact with the data.

This first program created a simple menu containing five choice options. Selecting a choice triggered a specific event. This program is the result of the specific event. In this project, your program will create the specific event for choice (or command button) #1—Add A New Record.

### Step 1: Start Your Compiler

Start your compiler, if necessary.

### Step 2: Create a New Project

Open the **File** menu and click **New Project**. In the New Project dialog box, double-click the **Standard EXE** button. Your VB environment should look like Figure 2-7.

**FIGURE 2-7**
Starting a new project

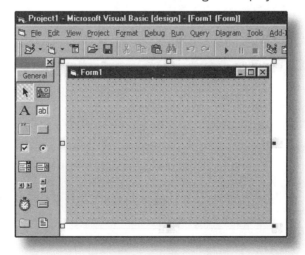

## Step 3: Add Your Controls

Now let's place your controls. Place six label controls, six text box controls, and two command button controls as shown in Figure 2-8. Size each control and the form so that they are the approximate size of those shown in the figure. Position the form in the middle of the Form Layout window. Change the appropriate properties for each control as outlined in the following chart. Choose an appropriate ForeColor, BackColor, and Font for the lblHeading control.

| Control | Name | Caption |
|---------|------|---------|
| Project | Project2_3 | None |
| Form | frmDataInput | Data Input |
| Label1 | lblHeading | Add Record |
| Label2 | lblFname | Enter First Name |
| Label3 | lblMI | Enter Middle Initial |
| Label4 | lblLname | Enter Last Name |
| Label5 | lblPhone | Enter Phone Number |
| Label6 | lblDOB | Enter Date Of Birth |
| Command1 | cmdEnter | Enter |
| Command2 | cmdExit | Exit |
| Text1 | txtFname | No text (Caption is not a text box property) |
| Text2 | txtMI | No text (Caption is not a text box property) |
| Text3 | txtLname | No text (Caption is not a text box property) |
| Text4 | txtPhone | No text (Caption is not a text box property) |
| Text5 | txtDOB | No text (Caption is not a text box property) |
| Text6 | txtOutput | No text (Caption is not a text box property) |

**FIGURE 2-8**

Adding controls to a form

### Step 4: Save Your Project

Open the **File** menu and click **Save Project As**. In the Save File As dialog box, select the folder and/or disk to which you are saving course files, and change the default file name to **DataInput**, which is the same name given to the form. Then click the **Save** button.

Once the form file is saved, the Save Project As dialog box opens. Make sure you are in the course files folder, and name the project **Project 2-3**. Then click the **Save** button. Once the project is saved, the information displayed in the Project window should look the same as in Figure 2-8.

### Step 5: Add Your Code to the Event

In this project you have two command buttons. One button will *Enter* the data input by the user. The other will *Exit* the Data Input form. In reality, when the Enter button is clicked, the data input by the user would be saved to an array or to a file. We will explore the tools needed to save the data to an array or database in later lessons. For now the data input will be displayed in the txtOutput text box at the bottom of the form.

You will need to double-click each command button in order to enter the necessary code for each event. The Form window editing area will open to display the code attached to each command button. Figure 2-9 shows where each line of the code should be entered for each command button.

**FIGURE 2-9**

Code to attach to each command button

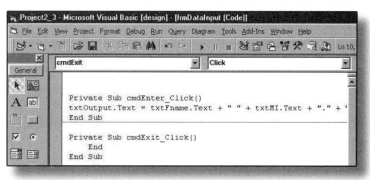

It is now up to you to add the appropriate lines of code. The following line of code is for the Enter button. After keying, this line of code will be too long to read at one time. You will need to use your arrow keys to scroll through the entire line.

```
txtOutput.Text = txtFname.Text + " " + txtMI.Text + "." + " " +
txtLname.Text + " " + txtPhone.Text + " " + txtDOB.Text
```

Once you type this line in, make sure you save both the form and the project again. Simply click the **Save** button on the toolbar.

Add the following code to the Exit button:

```
End
```

Again save your project after typing in this line of code.

Now you can run your program.

**2 9**

**Step 6: Run the Program**

Click the **Run** button on the toolbar to run the program. Your program should open in the middle of the screen. Type in a person's first name, middle initial, last name, phone number, and date of birth. Then click the **Enter** button. The data you entered should be displayed in the txtOutput text box at the bottom of the form. Remember that you will make this form functional once you learn about the additional tools needed to do so in later lessons. When you finish with the text input, test the Exit button to make sure your program exits.

**Step 7: Review Your Code**

Now that your program has run successfully, answer the following questions. Review your answers with your classmates and teacher.

**1.** Explain the purpose of a label.

_____

**2.** List at least three uses for labels.

_____

_____

_____

**3.** Explain the purpose of a data input form.

_____

_____

**4.** Explain the following line of code.

```
txtOutput.Text = txtFname.Text + " " + txtMI.Text + "." + " " +
txtLname.Text + " " + txtPhone.Text + " " + txtDOB.Text
```

_____

_____

_____

**5.** Explain why you used an Exit command button when the user can exit the program by clicking on the Close (X) button in the upper right corner of the window.

_____

_____

**6.** Explain the overall execution of the program.

_____

_____

_____

You now have a working data input program and are well on your way to being able to create user-friendly VB programs.

# *Summary*

This lesson introduced you to user interfaces. As you know, the easier a program is to use, the less likely it is that errors will occur when it is used.

User interfaces provide users with a selection of choices that allow them to interact easily with your program. You want to give them the control they need to proceed through your program at their own pace.

But you also maintain control through the code that sits behind your command buttons. In this lesson you created a simple menu program that gave the user a variety of choices, including an easy way out of the program. You then enhanced the menu to make it attractive to the user. You then created a data input form and designed it to be easy for the user to input information in a file.

## LESSON 2 REVIEW QUESTIONS

### SHORT ANSWER

**Define the following in the space provided.**

1. User interaction

   _____

2. Program design

   _____

   _____

3. End users

   _____

4. Program interface

   _____

   _____

5. Functionality

   _____

   _____

   _____

6. User friendly

   _____

   _____

   _____

   _____

**7.** Event

_____

_____

**8.** Controls

_____

_____

**9.** Properties

_____

_____

_____

**10.** Database

_____

_____

_____

**11.** Trigger

_____

**12.** Font

_____

_____

**13.** ForeColor

_____

**14.** Aesthetics

_____

_____

_____

## WRITTEN QUESTIONS

**Write your answers to the following questions in the space provided.**

**1.** Explain why it is important for a program to be user friendly.

_____

_____

**2.** Explain why control colors should be consistent with colors of similar applications.

_____

_____

_____

**3.** Explain the importance of using a program interface.

_____

_____

**4.** Explain how the programmer can maintain control through the user of a user interface.

_____

_____

_____

**5.** Explain the following color value - &H00FFFF00&. What color is this?

_____

## TESTING YOUR SKILLS

### APPLICATION 2-1

**SCANS**

In Project 2-1 you created a simple menu program. In Project 2-3 you created a data input program that could be the result of clicking the #1 command button on the simple menu. In this application you will design a form that could be used for *modifying* an existing record. This is the #2 command button on the simple menu.

When you modify a record, you first need to allow the user to select a record and then display the record so that the user can decide whether it is the correct record to be modified. If it is the correct record, then the user will be allowed to modify it.

Create a form within a project that is simply a layout of the form to be used for this application. Save the form as **ModForm**, and save the project as **App2-1**.

Do not code the command buttons. The proper functionality will be added in later lessons.

## APPLICATION 2-2

In this application you will design a form that could be used for *deleting* an existing record. This is the #3 command button on the simple menu you created in Project 2-1.

When you delete a record, you first need to allow the user to select a record and then display the record so that the user can decide whether it is the correct record to be deleted. If it is the correct record, then the user will be allowed to delete it.

Create a form within a project that is simply a layout of the form to be used for this application. Save the form as **DelForm**, and save the project as **App2-2**.

Do not code the command buttons.

## APPLICATION 2-3

In this application you will design a form that could be used for *viewing/printing* an existing record. This is the #4 command button on the simple menu you created in Project 2-1.

When you view/print a record, you first need to allow the user to select a record and then display the record so that the user can decide whether it is the correct record to be viewed or printed. If it is the correct record, then the user will be allowed to view/print it. You may also want to give the user the choice between viewing or printing by adding separate command buttons.

Create a form within a project that is simply a layout of the form to be used for this application. Save the form as **ViewForm**, and save the project as **App2-3**.

Do not code the command buttons.

## CRITICAL THINKING

 Estimated Time: 2 hours

In this lesson we focused on user interfaces. We created a simple menu and a variety of forms to be used as selections from the simple menu. However, as was mentioned throughout the lesson, a variety of different user interfaces can be created for a variety of programs.

Your assignment is to create two additional user interfaces, different from those included in this lesson. Use the following questions as guides for creating these additional interfaces.

1. What kind of information will I be collecting from the users?

2. Is there a logical flow to the collection of the information?

3. What do I want the user to be able to do with the information?

Once you have answered these questions, you should have an idea of the type of interface you need to create.

# CALCULATIONS AND MULTIPLE FORMS

## OBJECTIVES

**Upon completion of this lesson, you should be able to:**

- Explain the purpose of calculations.

- Explain the advantages and disadvantages of performing calculations vs. storing values.

- Demonstrate the appropriate use of calculations vs. storing values.

- Demonstrate the proper use of variables in calculations.

- Relate your calculations to user interaction.

- Translate math formulas into code.

- Design code for including calculations in programs.

- Understand precedence and distinguish between the order of operations.

- Organize projects with multiple forms.

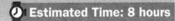 **Estimated Time: 8 hours**

## Introduction

Calculations are an important part of any computer program. Computers are always calculating something. It may be interest on a past due invoice, or a company's weekly payroll, or maybe sports statistics. In fact, computers are often thought of as "super calculators."

The main purpose of a calculation is to find an answer. Users need to know something, so they ask the computer to perform the calculation for them. Why? Because the computer does it faster, and if it is programmed right, it will not make a mistake. Just like with other user interfaces, calculations help make life easier for the user.

This lesson will focus on the following:

- **Understanding the purpose of calculations.** We continuously explain the purpose behind including calculations in code. It is not enough to know how; you also need to know why.

- **The advantages and disadvantages of performing calculations vs. storing values, and the appropriate use of calculations vs. storing values.** When you develop code for a program, you will notice there are instances in which the calculation is performed and the answer is output, but the answer is never stored. Some calculations are so simple and quick that it makes more sense to perform the calculation when the answer is needed than to store the answer again and again in a file. For example, if you know that an employee worked 36 regular hours and 0 overtime hours, then you know the total hours, or you can calculate it very quickly.

- **The proper use of variables in calculations and how to relate calculations to user interaction.** As just mentioned, you will be performing calculations needed by the end user. Therefore, you will need to gather information from the end user in order to perform the calculation so that it benefits that particular end user. The only way to get input from the end user is to use variables through a user interface, and these variables need to be defined and used properly.

- **Translating math formulas into code, designing code for including calculations in programs, and distinguishing precedence among the order of operators.** These three objectives basically translate into programming. You will decide what calculations you need to perform, and then you will find the appropriate math formula. At that point, you will begin to translate the formula into code. You will need to pay particular attention to precedence in order to make sure complex formulas are performed correctly.

- **Organizing your projects with multiple forms.** You will be able to include multiple calculations in your projects by coding them on to the same form. However, it makes better sense to place each calculation on its own form. This allows you to organize your programs in a form that users will expect.

## PROJECT 3-1 : Foreign Currency Conversion Ⓑ

Your first project is to create a program that converts foreign currency into dollars. You have all heard the saying "the world is becoming a smaller place," and getting information from one country to another is very easy. Many businesses, both large and small, are developing a global customer base. One concern in the financial world is the conversion of foreign currencies into dollars and vice versa. What makes this calculation difficult is the fact that currency values change daily.

This first program converts foreign currencies into dollars. You begin focusing on the proper use of *variables* and the proper structure of *calculations* in this project. You will be expected to exercise more control over the development of your programs beginning in this lesson.

### Step 1: Start Your Compiler

Start your compiler, if necessary.

### Step 2: Create a New Project

Open the **File** menu and click **New Project**. In the New Project dialog box, double-click the **Standard EXE** button. The Project1 file opens, displaying a blank form named Form1.

## Step 3: Add Your Controls

Resize your form so that it looks like Figure 3-1. Notice that the project and form are numbered 1 by default. You will change the names, captions, and other properties later.

FIGURE 3-1
Changing the size of the form

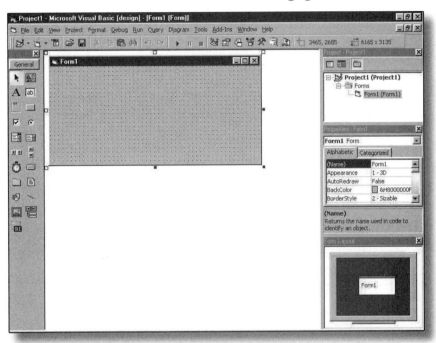

Now let's place your controls. Place five label controls, one command button, and three text box controls as shown on Figure 3-2. Size the controls and the form so that they are the approximate size of those shown in the figure. Position the form in the middle of the Form Layout window. Change the appropriate properties for each control as outlined in the following chart. Notice that the names used for labels and their related text boxes are almost identical. The only difference is the **prefix**.

| Control | Property | Value |
| --- | --- | --- |
| Project | Name | Project3_1 |
| Form | Name | frmForeignConvert |
| | Caption | Foreign Currency/Conversion |
| Label1 | Name | lblForeign |
| | Alignment | Left Justify |
| | Caption | Amount in Foreign Currency |
| Label2 | Name | lblCurrName |
| | Alignment | Left Justify |
| | Caption | Currency Name |
| Label3 | Name | lblRate |
| | Alignment | Left Justify |
| | Caption | Currency Rate |
| Label4 | Name | lblDollars |
| | Alignment | Left Justify |
| | Caption | Amount in Dollars |

**3 7**

| Label5 | Name | LblDollarAmt |
| | Alignment | Right Justify |
| | BackColor | &H0000FF00& (Green) |
| | Caption | None |
| Command1 | Name | cmdConvert |
| | Caption | Convert |
| Text1 | Name | txtForeign |
| | Alignment | Right Justify |
| | Text | None |
| Text2 | Name | txtCurrName |
| | Alignment | Left Justify |
| | Text | None |
| Text3 | Name | txtRate |
| | Alignment | Right Justify |
| | Text | None |

**FIGURE 3-2**
Placing controls on the form

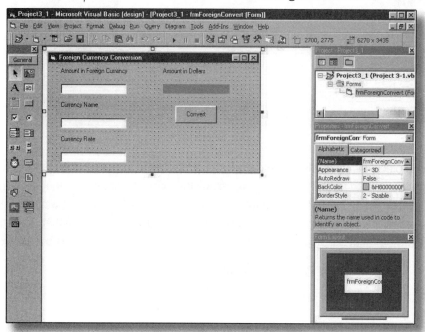

### Step 4: Save Your Project

Open the **File** menu and click **Save Project As**. In the Save File As dialog box, change the default file name to **ForeignConvert**, which is the same name given to the form. This is a good way to ensure consistency. Select the folder and/or disk containing your course files. Then click the **Save** button.

Once the form file is saved, the Save Project As dialog box opens. Make sure you are saving to the same course folder. Then rename the project to **Project 3-1**. Click the **Save** button. Once the project is saved, the information displayed in the Project window should look the same as in Figure 3-2.

Remember to save your projects often!

## Step 5: Add Your Code to the Event

You now need to add the code to the control that will trigger the event. For this project, you will also add code to the **declarations section** of the form, which is used to declare variables and **general-purpose code**. General-purpose code is code that is performed separately from any control. At this point you will be using the declarations section to declare variables.

*Variables* are temporary storage areas in memory. These store data so that they can be manipulated quickly and efficiently. You are responsible for *declaring* and naming your variables. The *Dim* statement is used to declare a variable. The variable should be explicitly declared as one of the VB *data types*. If it is not declared as a specific type, the variable becomes a *Variant* data type by default.

Variables also need to be named. That is your responsibility! Variable names should begin with a three-letter prefix that designates the data type. For example, an *integer* should begin with *int,* a *string* with *str,* and *currency* with *cur.* You will use these *naming conventions* from this point forward.

Add the code shown in Figure 3-3 to your declarations section and your command button.

**FIGURE 3-3**
Declarations section and command button code

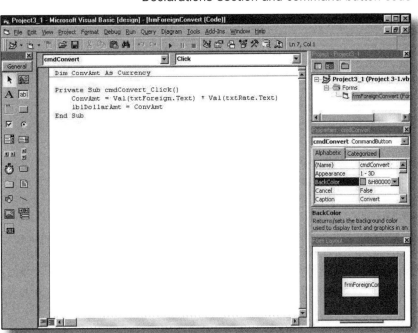

Your program should now be ready to run.

## Step 6: Run the Program

Click the **Run** button on the toolbar to run your program. Your program should open in the middle of the screen.

Now enter values to test the program. The user is required to enter an amount of a foreign currency in the *Amount in Foreign Currency* text box. In the *Currency Name* text box, the user will input the name of the currency that he or she is holding. For example, French currency would be francs, Japanese currency, yen, and so forth.

In the *Currency Rate* text box, the user is required to enter the daily exchange rate for the specified currency. Exchange rates can be found in local newspapers' financial sections. The exchange rates in the following chart are sample rates. You should be able to find actual, current rates in your local paper, on the Internet, or by calling your local bank.

| Currency | Foreign Currency in $ | $ in Foreign Currency |
| --- | --- | --- |
| Dollar (Canadian) | .6562 | 1.5239 |
| Yen (Japan) | .008671 | 115.33 |
| Peso (Mexico) | .100503 | 9.9500 |
| Mark (Germany) | .6024 | 1.6601 |

For this calculation, the user should enter the value from the *Foreign Currency in $* column in the *Currency Rate* text box and then press **Convert**. The correct amount in dollars should appear in the green label, and it should be a currency data type that displays four decimal places.

### Step 7: Review Your Code

Review your code by answering the following questions. Review your answers with your classmates and teacher.

**1.** Compare the names of the related labels and text boxes. Explain the differences or similarities.

_____

_____

_____

_____

**2.** Why did you use a label control instead of a text box to display the answer?

_____

_____

_____

**3.** Explain why the BackColor property was changed to green.

_____

_____

**4.** Explain why the text box Alignment properties are set the way they are.

_____

_____

**5.** Is the ConvAmt variable named properly? Explain your answer.

_____

_____

_____

**6.** Explain why the lblDollarAmt displays four decimal places (at most) when its Caption property is assigned the value of a variable declared as a Currency data type.

_____

_____

**7.** Explain the following line of code.

```
Dim ConvAmt As Currency
```

_____

_____

**8.** Explain the result of the above line of code being placed in the declarations section.

_____

_____

_____

**9.** Explain the following lines of code.

```
Private Sub cmdConvert_Click()
    ConvAmt = Val(txtForeign.Text) * Val(txtRate.Text)
    lblDollarAmt = ConvAmt
End Sub
```

_____

_____

_____

_____

_____

_____

**10.** Explain the overall execution of the program.

_____

_____

_____

_____

_____

# PROJECT 3-2:
## Developing an Additional Calculation

In this project you will add another calculation to the Project 3-1 form. This calculation will be the reverse of the one you created in Project 3-1. In other words, you will convert U.S. dollars into a foreign currency.

### Step 1: Start Your Compiler

Start your compiler, if necessary.

### Step 2: Open Project 3-1

Open the **File** menu and click **Open Project**. In the Open Project dialog box, click either the **Existing** or **Recent** tab and open **Project 3-1**.

### Step 3: Add Your Controls

The first thing you should do is save both your project and form. Save the project as **Project 3-2**. Remember that you should resave the form also to make it separate from the form used in Project 3-1. Save the *ForeignConvert* form as **ForeignConvert2**. Then resize your form to approximately twice its current size.

Now add the necessary controls for the second calculation. You should make an effort to separate the two calculations by more than just blank space. **Frame controls** can be used for just that purpose—passive separation. Frames can be used to group controls that belong together. The Frame control also has a Caption property, which means that you can place a different "title" on each group of controls instead of relying totally on the Form caption. Use a Frame control to organize your multiple purpose form. (*Hint*: You will need to create the Frame first and then add controls to it. Most controls *cannot* be clicked and dragged onto a Frame after they are created; the Frame must be created first. Make this your usual practice!)

Use the following table to record the controls you add and the property values you change.

| Control | Property | Value |
|---------|----------|-------|
|         |          |       |
|         |          |       |
|         |          |       |
|         |          |       |
|         |          |       |
|         |          |       |
|         |          |       |
|         |          |       |
|         |          |       |
|         |          |       |
|         |          |       |
|         |          |       |
|         |          |       |
|         |          |       |
|         |          |       |
|         |          |       |
|         |          |       |
|         |          |       |
|         |          |       |
|         |          |       |
|         |          |       |
|         |          |       |
|         |          |       |
|         |          |       |
|         |          |       |
|         |          |       |

### Step 4: Save Your Project

Make sure you save both your form and project one additional time before running your program.

### Step 5: Run Your Program

The program should run exactly as it did in Project 3-1. The only difference is that the form now displays two working calculations. Make sure you test your program using the *$ in Foreign Currency* information from Project 3-1.

If you would like, you can modify this program by changing fonts and color schemes. Please remember that the user expects consistency, so do not go wild with your color selections!

### Step 6: Review Your Code

When your program runs successfully, review your code with your classmates and teacher.

---

## P R O J E C T   3 - 3 :
## Another Multiple Calculation Form

In this project you will create another form containing multiple calculations. The calculations you create on this form will convert your height in feet and inches into centimeters and meters.

### Step 1: Start Your Compiler

Start your compiler, if necessary.

### Step 2: Create a New Project

Open the **File** menu and click **New Project**. When the New Project window appears, double-click the **Standard EXE** button. The Project1 file opens, displaying a blank form named Form1.

### Step 3: Add Your Controls

Now let's place your controls. Place seven label controls, two text box controls, one command button control, and one VScrollBar control as shown on Figure 3-4. Size each control and the form so that they are the approximate size of those shown in the figure. Position the form in the middle of the Form Layout window. Change the appropriate properties for each control as outlined in the following chart.

There is one new control and a new control property that need to be brought to your attention. The new control property is *TabIndex*. TabIndex sets the order in which the controls react to the Tab key. A control with a TabIndex property equal to 1 will be the first control highlighted. A control with a TabIndex of 2 will be the second, and so on. This is useful because many users like to use the Tab key when moving from one input control to the next.

**FIGURE 3-4**
Placing controls on the form

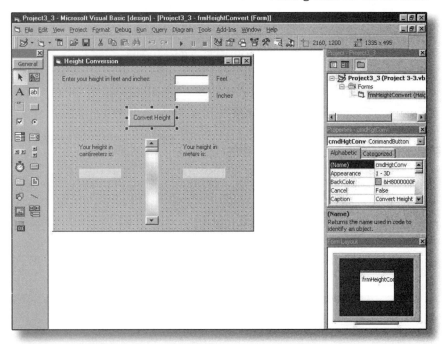

The new control is the **VScrollBar**. This scroll bar is a vertical scroll bar. A vertical scroll bar indicates to the user that more data are present below the bottom edge of the screen. The scroll bar is used to bring more data into view. In this project, you will use the vertical scroll bar for a different purpose. Your scroll bar will provide an estimate of where your height falls in a given range. You will provide the information necessary to the scroll bar control through preset properties and assignments to properties in your code.

| Control | Property | Value |
| --- | --- | --- |
| Project | Name | Project3_3 |
| Form | Name | frmHeightConvert |
| | Caption | Height Conversion |
| Label1 | Name | lblEnterInfo |
| | Alignment | Left Justify |
| | Caption | Enter your height in feet and inches: |
| Label2 | Name | lblFeet |
| | Alignment | Left Justify |
| | Caption | Feet |
| Label3 | Name | lblInches |
| | Alignment | Left Justify |
| | Caption | Inches |
| Label4 | Name | lblCent |
| | Alignment | Left Justify |
| | Caption | Your height in centimeters is: |

| Label5 | Name | lblMtr |
| | Alignment | Left Justify |
| | Caption | Your height in meters is: |
| Label6 | Name | lblCentValue |
| | BackColor | &H0080FFFF& (Light Yellow) |
| | Caption | None |
| Label7 | Name | lblMtrValue |
| | BackColor | &H0080FFFF& (Light Yellow) |
| | Caption | None |
| VScrollBar1 | Name | vscrHeight |
| | Max | 0 |
| | Min | 275 |
| | Value | 275 |
| Command1 | Name | cmdHgtConv |
| | Caption | Convert Height |
| | TabIndex | 3 |
| Text1 | Name | txtFeet |
| | Alignment | Right Justify |
| | TabIndex | 1 |
| | Text | None |
| Text2 | Name | txtInches |
| | Alignment | Right Justify |
| | TabIndex | 2 |
| | Text | None |

### Step 4: Save Your Project

Open the **File** menu and click **Save Project As**. In the Save File As dialog box, change the default file name to **HeightConvert**, which is the same name given to the form. This is a good way to ensure consistency. Select the folder and/or disk containing your course files. Then click the **Save** button.

Once the form file is saved, the Save Project As dialog box opens. Make sure you are saving to the same course folder. Then rename the project to **Project 3-3**. Click the **Save** button. Once the project is saved, the information displayed in the Project window should look the same as in Figure 3-4.

Remember to save your projects often!

### Step 5: Add Your Code to the Event

You now need to add the code to the control that will trigger the event. For this project you will again be adding variable declarations to the declarations section of the form. Remember that you need to name your variables and declare them as a specific data type. Your variable names should begin with a three-letter prefix that designates the variable data type.

Add the code shown in Figure 3-5 to your declarations section and to your command button.

**FIGURE 3-5**

Declarations section and command button code

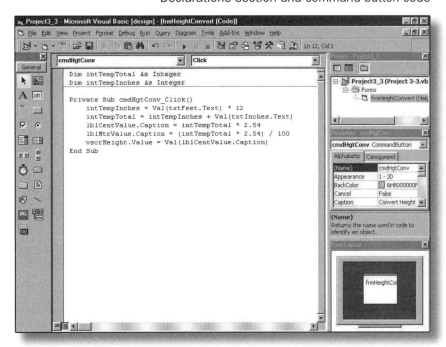

Once you type in your code, make sure you save both the form and the project again. Now you can run your program.

### Step 6: Run the Program

Click the **Run** button on the toolbar to run your program. Your program should open in the middle of the screen. Enter your height in feet and inches. Because of the TabIndex properties being set, you can tab between the text boxes and the command button. After you enter your height, click on the **Convert Height** command button. Your height will be converted to both centimeters and meters in the yellow labels. The vertical scroll bar will place its scroll button at your approximate height on the "scale."

### Step 7: Review Your Code

When your program runs successfully, answer the following questions. Review your answers with your classmates and teacher.

**1.** Explain why the labels are usually left justified and the text boxes are usually right justified in your programs.

_____

_____

_____

_____

_____

**2.** Explain why you use labels for your final answers.

_____

_____

_____

**4 7**

**3.** Explain your use of the VScrollBar control.

_____

_____

_____

**4.** Explain why the VScrollBar Max property is set to 0 and the Min property is set to 275.

_____

_____

_____

_____

**5.** Explain the meaning of the VScrollBar range being 0 to 275.

_____

_____

_____

_____

**6.** Explain why the initial value of the VScrollBar Value property is set to 275.

_____

_____

_____

**7.** Explain the purpose of the TabIndex property.

_____

_____

_____

_____

**8.** Explain the following variable declaration statements

```
Dim intTempTotal As Integer
Dim intTempInches As Integer
```

_____

_____

_____

**9.** Explain the following block of code.

```
Private Sub cmdHgtConv_Click()
    intTempInches = Val(txtFeet.Text) * 12
    intTempTotal = intTempInches + Val(txtInches.Text)
    lblCentValue.Caption = intTempTotal * 2.54
    lblMtrValue.Caption = (intTempTotal * 2.54) / 100
    vscrHeight.Value = Val(lblCentValue.Caption)
End Sub
```

_____

_____

_____

_____

**10.** Explain the overall execution of the program.

_____

_____

_____

_____

_____

_____

You have not only performed additional calculations, but now you are manipulating multiple variables and additional controls and properties. You are beginning to see the power of Visual Basic.

## PROJECT 3-4:
## Short-Term Simple Interest Loan

In this project you will create one last calculation form. The calculation you create on this form will compute the simple interest on money borrowed over a short-term time period. Many businesses and individuals borrow various amounts of money for short time periods in order to meet certain financial obligations. They then pay this money back, usually in a number of months, with simple interest added on. Simple interest is interest that is calculated on the principal (the amount borrowed) only; there is no compounding (charging interest on interest) involved as with long-term borrowing.

In this project, we will discuss **precedence**. Precedence is the order in which **operators** are applied within a formula. This order is the same as in algebra. Operations are performed in the following order:

( )

^

*, /, \ Mod

+ or −

It is important to know in which order these operators are applied. If you do not pay attention to precedence, you will end up with an arithmetic calculation or other operation that does *not* do what you expect! Use parentheses to establish which operations are carried out first. Because the operators inside parentheses are applied first, simply use parentheses to segregate the portions of your multiple calculations. Parentheses also help make your code more readable. Anyone looking at code will find it easier to follow if your calculations, at least the harder ones, are segregated with parentheses.

### Step 1: Start Your Compiler

Start your compiler, if necessary.

### Step 2: Create a New Project

Open the **File** menu and click **New Project**. In the New Project dialog box, double-click the **Standard EXE** button. The Project1 file opens, displaying a blank form named Form1.

### Step 3: Add Your Controls

Now let's place your controls. Place five label controls, three text box controls, and one command button control as shown in Figure 3-6. Size each control and the form so that they are the approximate size of those shown in the figure. Position the form in the middle of the Form Layout window. Change the appropriate properties for each control as outlined in the following chart.

**FIGURE 3-6**

Placing controls on the form

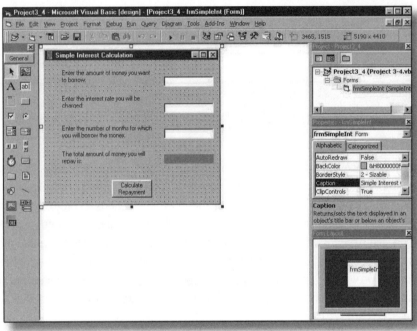

One additional Form property that you will use in this project is the *Icon* property. The Icon property allows you to place an icon in the upper left corner of the form. The one used for this project is the Calculator icon. (If you are using Visual Studio 6.0, the icon has been saved to the Student Data & Resources files included on the *Electronic Instructor* CD accompanying this book.)

If you are not using Visual Studio 6.0, then you will need to ask your teacher for the appropriate icon.

| Control | Property | Value |
|---------|----------|-------|
| Project | Name | Project3_4 |
| Form | Name | frmSimpleInt |
| | Caption | Simple Interest Calculation |

|  |  |  |
|---|---|---|
|  | Icon | Calc.ico |
| Label1 | Name | lblPrincipal |
|  | Alignment | Left Justify |
|  | Caption | Enter the amount of money you want to borrow: |
| Label2 | Name | lblIntRate |
|  | Alignment | Left Justify |
|  | Caption | Enter the interest rate you will be charged: |
| Label3 | Name | lblMonths |
|  | Alignment | Left Justify |
|  | Caption | Enter the number of months for which you will borrow the money: |
| Label4 | Name | lblAnswer |
|  | Alignment | Left Justify |
|  | Caption | The total amount of money you will repay is: |
| Label5 | Name | lblRepay |
|  | Alignment | Right Justify |
|  | BackColor | &H0000FF00& (Green) |
|  | Caption | None |
| Command1 | Name | cmdCalcRepay |
|  | Caption | Calculate Repayment |
|  | TabIndex | 4 |
| Text1 | Name | txtPrincipal |
|  | Alignment | Right Justify |
|  | TabIndex | 1 |
|  | Text | None |
| Text2 | Name | txtIntRate |
|  | Alignment | Right Justify |
|  | TabIndex | 2 |
|  | Text | None |
| Text3 | Name | txtMonths |
|  | Alignment | Right Justify |
|  | TabIndex | 3 |
|  | Text | None |

## Step 4: Save Your Project

Open the **File** menu and click **Save Project As**. In the Save File As dialog box, change the default file name to **SimpleInt**, which is the same name given to the form. This is a good way to ensure consistency. Select the folder and/or disk containing your course files. Then click the **Save** button.

Once the form file is saved, the Save Project As dialog box opens. Make sure you are saving to the same course folder. Then rename the project to **Project 3-4**. Click the **Save** button. Once the project is saved, the information displayed in the Project window should look the same as in Figure 3-6.

Remember to save your projects often!

## Step 5: Add Your Code to the Event

You now need to add the code to the control that will trigger the event. You will again be adding variable declarations to the declarations section of the form. Remember that you need to name your variables and declare them as a specific data type. Your variable names should begin with a three-letter prefix that designates the variable data type.

Add the code shown in Figure 3-7 to your declarations section. The complete code for the command button is shown following Figure 3-7.

**FIGURE 3-7**
Declarations section and partial command button code

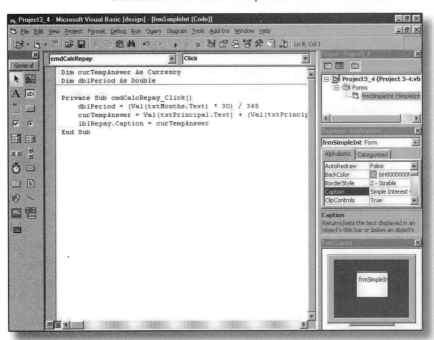

Add the following code for the command button:

```
Private Sub cmdCalcRepay_Click()
    dblPeriod = (Val(txtMonths.Text) * 30) / 365
    curTempAnswer = Val(txtPrincipal.Text) +
        (Val(txtPrincipal.Text) * ((Val(txtIntRate.Text) / 100)
        * dblPeriod))
    lblRepay.Caption = curTempAnswer
End Sub
```

Once you type in your code, make sure you save both the form and the project again. Now you can run your program.

## Step 6: Run the Program

Click the **Run** button on the toolbar to run your program. Your program should open in the middle of the screen. Enter an amount you would like to borrow, the interest rate the bank will charge you, and the number of months for which you will borrow the money. Click the **Calculate Repayment** command button, and the repayment amount will display in the green label.

## Step 7: Review Your Code

When your program runs successfully, answer the following questions. Review your answers with your classmates and teacher.

**1.** Explain the benefit of using parentheses in your calculations and formulas.

_____

_____

_____

**2.** Explain why you do not set the TabIndex property for every control.

_____

_____

**3.** Explain your use of the Calculator icon.

_____

_____

_____

**4.** Explain the following variable declaration statements:

```
Dim curTempAnswer As Currency
Dim dblPeriod As Double
```

_____

_____

_____

_____

**5.** Explain why the preceding variables have the proper prefixes.

_____

_____

_____

**6.** Explain the following block of code.

```
Private Sub cmdCalcRepay_Click()
    dblPeriod = (Val(txtMonths.Text) * 30) / 365
    curTempAnswer = Val(txtPrincipal.Text) +
        (Val(txtPrincipal.Text) * ((Val(txtIntRate.Text) / 100)
        * dblPeriod))
    lblRepay.Caption = curTempAnswer
End Sub
```

_____

_____

_____

_____

_____

**7.** Explain the overall execution of the program.

_____

_____

_____

_____

You have now created multiple forms that perform multiple calculations. In the next project you will combine them all.

## P R O J E C T   3 - 5 : One Project, Multiple Forms

In this project, you will add all the forms to one project and then create a menu that will allow you to run any calculation you choose.

### Step 1: Start Your Compiler

Start your compiler, if necessary.

### Step 2: Create a New Project

Open the **File** menu and click **New Project**. In the New Project dialog box, double-click the **Standard EXE** button. The Project1 file opens, displaying a blank form named Form1.

**Step 3: Create a Menu Form**

**1.** Create a menu form that provides a choice for each of the calculations you programmed in this lesson. Also remember to add an Exit button. In the following space, sketch the layout of your menu form.

In addition to creating the form, you will need to make sure that this project uses your menu form as the Start Up form. This is detailed in Step 5.

**Step 4: Add Code to Your Menu Buttons**

Each menu button should cause one of your programs from this lesson to execute. Each program is basically the form used in that particular project. Therefore, the code for each button should be similar to the following:

```
Private Sub cmdHeightCalc_Click()
    frmHeightConvert.Show
End Sub
```

This is the code that will execute the Height Conversion form you created in Project 3-3. All you need to add inside the body of each command button is one line: **frmFormName.Show**. This line of code tells VB to show the form you have named in the code line. The **Show method** shows the form and allows the user to interact with it. Additional methods regarding multiple forms will be discussed in later lessons.

**1.** Add code to your menu buttons. Write your code for each menu button in the following space:

_____

_____

_____

_____

_____

_____

_____

_____

_____

_____

**Step 5: Add Additional Forms to the Project**

Now that your menu buttons are coded, you need to physically add each form to this project. Click **Project** on the Menu bar, and then select **Add Form**. In the Add Form dialog box, click the **Existing** tab. Select the folder that contains your forms for this lesson and choose each form one at a time. As you add each form, the form icon and form name should appear in the Project window.

**1.** List the forms added to your project in the space below.

_____

_____

_____

Click **Project** on the Menu bar and select **Project Name Properties**. In the Project Properties dialog box, make sure that **menu form** is the selected object in the *Startup Object* list box. The object selected in this list box is the one that executes when the project is run.

**Step 6: Save Your Project**

Click the **Save** button to save your project. Save your new form as **CalcMenu**; the foreign currency conversion form as **ForeignConvert2**, the height conversion form as **HeightConvert**; and the simple interest form as **SimpleInt**. Save your project as **Project 3-5**.

**Step 7: Run Your Program**

Click the **Run** button on the toolbar to execute your program.

The program should initially provide you with a menu that offers at least three calculations and an Exit button. Each menu button should "show," or execute, the form you assigned to that button. The Exit button should exit the project.

Each form should exit when you click on the **X** button in the upper right corner of the form. When each form exits, control of the program should return to the menu form. The only two choices that exit the entire program are the Exit button on the menu form and the X button.

You should now have a working menu with at least three attached working forms.

**Step 8: Review Your Code**

When your program runs successfully, review your project with your classmates and teacher.

# Performing Calculations vs. Storing Values

Should you perform calculations every time you need an answer, or should you save the answer for later use? This is a very important issue when performing calculations.

In the introduction to this lesson, we mentioned payroll as an example. If we know the regular hours worked and the overtime hours worked, we can calculate the total hours worked rather quickly. Because it is a simple calculation requiring very little processing time, we could probably get away with repeating the calculation every time we wanted the answer.

However, the best way to answer this question is to compare processing time to storage space. Will it be easier on your system to perform the calculation once and then store the answer? Or will it be easier to perform the calculation every time without storing the answer at all? The answer depends on the system and how the system administrator is trying to optimize the system's performance.

Your job is to make sure your programs help optimize the system or at least run within the established framework. And the best way to do this is to discuss things with your system administrator. In the world of *distributed processing*—computing that takes place on multiple machines in multiple locations—you as a programmer need to be aware of system *infrastructures* and system *capabilities*. Start learning now about systems by discussing things with your school's system administrator or technology coordinator.

# Summary

This lesson focused on calculations. You began with foreign currency conversions and then moved into more complex calculations. The one important feature of every program is the need to collect data from the user. As a programmer you will not know the needs of every user; therefore, you need to write your programs so that each user can get the desired solution.

This lesson also stressed variables: meaningful variable names, necessary variable types, and the use of variables within the program that the user never sees. These are all very important aspects of making your program readable.

You also learned about precedence. It is important that your calculations work correctly. If you are not aware of the order in which operations are carried out, then it is very likely that your calculations will not work correctly. Use parentheses to control the order of operations.

You also learned how to add forms to your programs. These can be added to any project.

## LESSON 3 REVIEW QUESTIONS

### SHORT ANSWER

**Define the following in the space provided.**

1. Variables

   _____

   _____

2. Calculations

   _____

**3.** Declarations section

_____

**4.** General-purpose code

_____

**5.** Declaring

_____

_____

**6.** Dim statement

_____

**7.** Data types

_____

**8.** Variant data type

_____

**9.** Integer

_____

**10.** String

_____

**11.** Currency

_____

_____

**12.** Naming convention

_____

_____

**13.** Frame control

_____

_____

**14.** TabIndex property

_____

**15.** VScrollBar

_____

_____

**16.** Precedence

_____

**17.** Operator

_____

**18.** Mod

_____

**19.** Icon property

_____

**20.** Show method

_____

**21.** Startup object

_____

**22.** Distributed processing

_____

_____

_____

**23.** Infrastructures

_____

_____

**24.** Capabilities

_____

## WRITTEN QUESTIONS

**Write your answers to the following questions in the space provided.**

**1.** Explain the proper way to name variables.

_____

_____

2. Explain in which section of code variables are declared.

_____

3. Explain general-purpose code.

_____

4. Explain why it is important to assign correct data types to variables.

_____

_____

5. Explain one use of the Frame control.

_____

_____

6. Explain the Show method.

_____

_____

7. Explain the use of a Startup object.

_____

8. What is the "trade-off" when deciding to store data or to simply re-run the calculation every time you need an answer?

_____

_____

_____

9. List and define the most common data types in VB.

_____

_____

_____

_____

_____

_____

_____

_____

_____

_____

_____

_____

_____

_____

_____

# TESTING YOUR SKILLS

## APPLICATION 3-1

In Project 3-4, you created a program that would calculate simple interest on a short-term loan. One alternative that banks give to customers who borrow short-term is to *discount* their loan. This means that the customer allows the bank to subtract the amount of interest from the loan proceeds (the amount of money the customer receives). Then when the customer repays the loan, they only have to repay the amount borrowed. For example, if you were to borrow $1,000 for 12 months at 10% interest, then you would owe the bank $1,100 when you repaid the loan. The interest would be $100. Discounting would allow you to pay the $100 interest up front. If you chose to do that, then you would only receive $900 from the bank ($1,000 - $100 interest). However, at the end of the 12 months, you would repay only the $1,000 because you had already paid the interest.

1. Open **Project 3-4**.

2. Save your form as **SimpleInt2** and your project as **App 3-1**.

3. Redesign the calculation so that the interest is subtracted.

4. Modify any labels, captions, or text that may confuse the user.

5. Save the modified code as **App 3-1**.

6. Run your program to test it. Debug it if necessary. Run it again.

## APPLICATION 3-2

In Project 2-1 you created a simple menu program. In Project 2-3 you created a data input program that could be the result of clicking the #1 command button on the simple menu. In App 2-1, App 2-2, and App 2-3, you created additional forms that could be the forms that each menu choice "points" to.

In this application you will add each of the forms created in the projects and applications just mentioned to Project 2-1.

1. Open **Project 2-1** and save it as **App 3-2**. Save the SimpleMenu form as **SimpleMenu2**.

2. Add each of the additional forms to the project. Save each form that you added with a modified name. Simply add a **2** to each name before saving it.

3. Modify the code for each menu button to show the appropriate form.

**6 1**

4. Save your forms and projects.

5. Remove the large text box from the bottom of the simple menu form. Remove the Exit buttons from every form *except* the simple menu form.

6. Run your programs to test them. Then debug them if necessary. Run them again.

## CRITICAL THINKING

Estimated Time: 4–6 hours

Create a list of calculations that will prove useful to you. In this lesson we discussed short-term loan calculations, foreign currency conversions, metric conversions, and numbering system conversions. Each profession has calculations that are useful on a daily basis.

Select a group of useful calculations and create forms for these calculations. For example, create a form or collection of forms for baseball statistics (batting average, ERA, slugging percentage, fielding percentage) or other sports statistics, grade calculations, exercise/workout records, or anything else of interest to you.

When you are finished creating the forms, create a "master" project that will contain all the forms you created. When you have created the master project and added all the forms, then create a menu form that will allow you to access each of the other forms from the menu.

When you are finished with the master project, you may want to create an executable file that will enable you to run your project on any computer.

# DECISION MAKING AND LOOPING

**Upon completion of this lesson, you should be able to:**

■ Define sequence, selection, and repetition control structures.

■ Explain the purpose of control structures.

■ Demonstrate the use of control structures.

■ Discriminate between the use of the various selection structures.

■ Discriminate between the use of the various repetition structures.

■ Design programs that utilize the various control structures.

🕐 **Estimated Time: 10 hours**

## Introduction

*Control structures* allow you to provide users with some control over your program. Rarely, if at all, will you find a program that allows the user to do just one thing. Programs give the user control over doing what they need to do when they would like to do it, and they allow the user to perform tasks multiple times.

There are three categories of control structures: *sequence*, *selection*, and *repetition*. Sequence control is usually found in a *top-down programming* environment, such as COBOL or C++. Visual Basic does not provide an overall top-down programming approach, so sequence control is not important in the overall design of the program. However, sequence control is important when coding your controls and *modules*.

Selection control enables you to allow the user to make choices. Selection is also referred to as *decision making*. You require the user to make a choice or selection. Then, based on that decision, your program executes a block of code or a form. You can add multiple selection structures to your programs.

There are three selection structures: *If*, *If/Else*, and *Select Case*. The If structure simply tests for a condition. If the condition is met, then something happens. If not, the program continues. The If/Else structure presents the user with a fork-in-the-road decision. If a condition is met, you follow one road; if the condition is not met, you follow the other road. The Select Case allows for a more structured, multiple selection to occur.

Repetition structures allow you to add *looping* to your programs. Looping simply means that a sequence of code repeats again and again until a condition is met. However, there is always the danger of entering a loop that cannot be exited. This is known as an *endless loop*—it goes on forever. You will be shown how to avoid this situation.

There are three repetition structures: *Do While*, *Do Until*, and *For*. The Do structures are built around the basis that a block of code will execute while or until a condition is met. The condition test can occur at the beginning of the block or at the end. The placement of the condition is very important. If the condition is placed at the beginning of the block, the code may never execute; if it is at the end, then the code will execute at least once. This will allow you to increase the usefulness of your program.

The For structure uses a counter to control its repetition. This type loop repeats a number of times determined by its *counter*, its *starting and ending loop values*, and its *increment*. The syntax of the For structure is more complicated but easy to understand once you begin to use it. The following is an example of the For structure syntax:

```
For counter = 1 To 10 Step 1
    lblDisplay.caption = "Hi there!"
Next
```

This For structure would loop 10 times, each time displaying the text "Hi there!" in the caption property of the label. Of course, this would happen so fast that you would see only the final "Hi there!" The *Next* clause tells the For loop to continue looping until it hits the upper limit of the loop counter, or 10.

The *Step* clause is unnecessary here because loops "step," or increment, by the *default value* of one. However, you now know that the Step clause is available should you wish to increment by more than one.

This lesson will focus on the following:

■ **Defining and explaining the purpose of control structures.** You will learn the seven different types of control structures and be able to explain their use.

■ **Demonstrating the use of control structures.** You will program multiple projects that will provide you with the opportunity to demonstrate the proper use of control structures.

■ **Discriminating between the use of the various selection and repetition structures.** You will design your programs using the various structures and various forms of those structures. By doing this you will gain the ability to decide which structure is the most appropriate for different situations.

■ **Designing programs that utilize the various controls.** Each lesson provides you with the opportunity to use these controls in new and existing programs.

## P R O J E C T   4 - 1 :
## CheckBox Control Using If Structure   Ⓑ

You have probably seen many programs that utilize *CheckBox* controls. These allow the user to make multiple choices at the same time. Each check box must be tested to determine whether it is checked. If so, something happens. If not, the box is ignored. We will use this control to introduce the If structure to you.

In this project you will modify the font conversion application you created in Application 1-3. The basic idea of this program is to take text entered by a user into a text box and then change the font as you did in Application 1-3. However, this time you will add check boxes for additional characteristics to be applied to the text.

### Step 1: Start Your Compiler

Start your compiler, if it is not already running.

### Step 2: Open App1-3

Open the **File** menu and click **Open Project**. From the Existing tab, open your **App1-3** project. Your VB environment should look like Figure 4-1.

**FIGURE 4-1**

App1-3 project

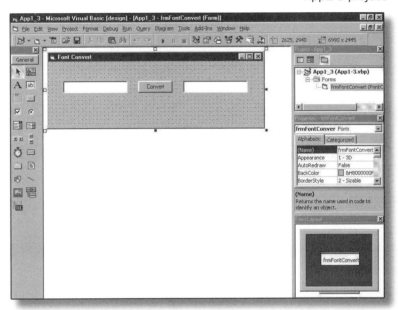

Save your form as **FontConvert2** and your project as **Project 4-1**.

### Step 3: Add Your Controls

Now resize your form and place your controls. Delete the **txtChanged** text box. Then place three CheckBox controls and one Label control as shown in Figure 4-2. Size the form and each control so that they are the approximate size of those shown in the figure. (*Hint:* The text boxes used for

**FIGURE 4-2**

Changing the size of the form and adding controls

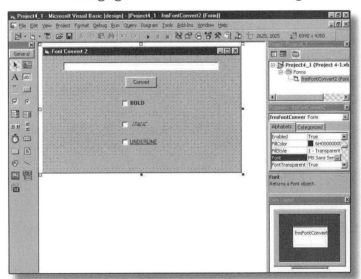

text should be just tall enough to hold the text. This adds to the aesthetics of the form.) Position the form in the middle of the Form Layout window.

Change the appropriate properties for each control as outlined in the following chart. The Project, Form, Textbox, and Command button are all from the original project. You will simply be changing the values of the properties for those controls listed in the chart. For the others, you will be starting from scratch. You will also notice that the name of the Command button from the original project had the wrong prefix. Make sure you correct it as shown in the chart.

| Control | Property | Value |
| --- | --- | --- |
| Project | Name | Project4_1 |
| Form | Name | frmFontConvert2 |
| | Caption | Font Convert 2 |
| Text1 | Name | txtNormal |
| | Font | MS Sans Serif, Regular, 8 |
| Command1 | Name | cmdConvert |
| | Caption | Convert |
| CheckBox1 | Name | chkBold |
| | Caption | BOLD |
| | Font | MS Sans Serif, Bold, 8 |
| CheckBox2 | Name | chkItalic |
| | Caption | ITALIC |
| | Font | MS Sans Serif, Italic, 8 |
| CheckBox3 | Name | chkUnderline |
| | Caption | UNDERLINE |
| | Font | MS Sans Serif, Regular, 8 |
| | | Underline option checked |
| Label1 | Name | lblChanged |
| | Caption | None |
| | Font | Courier, Regular, 10 |

When you click on the value of the **_Font property_**, an **_ellipsis ( . . . )_** will appear. Clicking on the ellipsis will cause the Font Dialog Box to open. This is where you will select the appropriate values for your Font property. See Figure 4-3.

**FIGURE 4-3**
Font Dialog Box

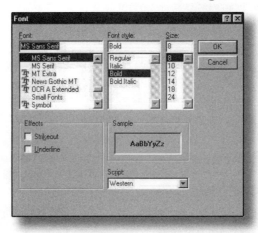

### Step 4: Save Your Project

Save your project changes by clicking the **Save** button on the toolbar.

### Step 5: Add Your Code to the Project

Now that your form and project have been designed, it is time to add the necessary code to the controls. With this project you will add code to the Command Button and to each CheckBox control.

Double-click the **command button** and modify the existing line of code between the "Private Sub" and "End Sub" lines of code to read as shown in the following gray box. Remember that your Command button was programmed for Application 1-3.

```
lblChanged.Caption = txtNormal.Text
```

Make sure you save both the form and the project again by clicking the **Save** button on the toolbar.

You now need to add code to the CheckBox controls. You will use If structures for each of the CheckBox controls to determine whether they are checked. First, double-click the **chkBold** CheckBox control. Enter the following lines of code between the existing "Private Sub" and "End Sub" lines of code.

```
If (chkBold.Value = 1) Then
    lblChanged.FontBold = True
End If
```

These lines of code perform as follows. If the condition in parentheses = 1, which means that the check box is checked, then the lblChanged FontBold property is set to True. This makes the font that is used for the label control appear in bold. The End If ends the If structure. Without the End If you would receive a *compile error*. The period (.) between the lblChanged property name and the FontBold property name denotes that the FontBold property belongs specifically to the lblChanged control.

You will notice that when you type in your code that VB actually assists you in selecting properties and values. If you type the name of your controls properly, a list box appears with the possible choice of properties or values for that type of control or property. If you simply type a portion of the property or value you want, then that item will be highlighted in the list. If you press the spacebar, then VB will insert the chosen item into your code for you. See Figure 4-4.

**67**

**FIGURE 4-4**
Property list box

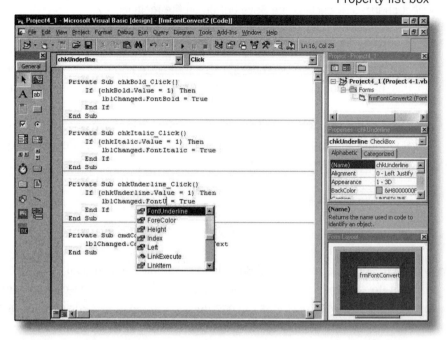

Now add the code necessary for the remaining two CheckBox controls, as shown in Figure 4-5.

**FIGURE 4-5**
Add code for two remaining CheckBox controls

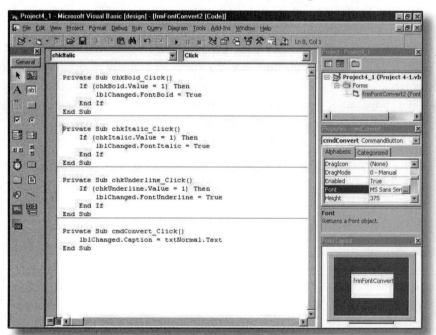

### Step 6: Run the Program

Click the **Run** button on the toolbar to run your program. Your program should open in the middle of the screen. Type a line of text into the text box. Select any of the check boxes or any combination of check boxes and then click the **convert** button. The text that you typed into the text box is now displayed on the label with the appropriate characteristics: **bold**, *italic*, and/or underlined. And it is displayed using the Courier font you assigned to its Font property.

If you followed the proceeding directions, then the program should work. However, type in a line of text, click the **convert** button, and then apply the characteristics you want. The characteristics are applied, but when you uncheck or deselect the box, the chosen characteristics are not removed. That is not the way you want your program to execute. We will modify this in the next project.

### Step 7: Review Your Code

Now that your program has run successfully (at least somewhat), answer the following questions. Review your answers with your classmates and teacher.

**1.** Explain the purpose of a CheckBox control.

**2.** Explain the purpose of using an If structure.

**3.** Explain how the If structure is used with the CheckBox control.

**4.** Explain the following block of code:

```
Private Sub chkItalic_Click()
    If (chkItalic.Value = 1) Then
        lblChanged.FontItalic = True
    End If
End Sub
```

**5.** From the code in question 4, explain why you are having the problem described at the end of Step 6.

**6.** Explain the overall execution of the program.

You are now able to use both check boxes and If structures. However, you have also been introduced to a shortcoming of the If structure through the problem presented at the end of Step 6. Next you will learn how to correct that problem.

## PROJECT 4-2 : If/Else Structure Ⓑ

In this project, you will correct the shortcomings of the If structure presented in Project 4-1 by using an If/Else structure. You will correct this problem through the simple addition of code.

The If structure simply tests for a condition. If the condition is met, then a body of code is performed. If the condition is *not* met, then the program simply moves on. That is why the problem occurred with unchecking the check boxes in the last project—there was no test to apply when it was unchecked.

### Step 1: Start Your Compiler

Start your compiler, if necessary.

### Step 2: Open Project 4-1

Open the **File** menu and click **Open Project**. From the **Existing** tab in the Open Project dialog box, open your **Project 4-1** project. Your VB environment should look like Figure 4-6.

**FIGURE 4-6**
Project 4-1

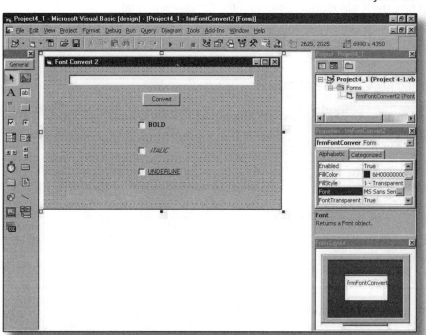

Save your form as **FontConvert3** and your project as **Project 4-2**.

### Step 3: Modify Your Controls

Change the properties of the following controls. Write the name of the value you choose in the space provided.

| Control | Property | Value |
|---------|----------|-------|
| Project | Name | _____ |
| Form | Name | _____ |
| | Caption | _____ |

The reason to change these names is to prevent major confusion between similar yet different projects and forms.

### Step 4: Add Code to Your CheckBox Controls

You will add the Else portion of the If/Else structure to each CheckBox control so that they perform as expected. You will be provided the code for one CheckBox control. It will be your responsibility to code the others.

Double-click the **BOLD** CheckBox. When the code window opens, modify your code to match the following:

```
Private Sub chkBold_Click()
    If (chkBold.Value = 1) Then
        lblChanged.FontBold = True
    Else: lblChanged.FontBold = False
    End If
End Sub
```

You will notice that one line of code has been added—the "Else" part of the If/Else structure. This line of code tells the program to *not* make the font bold if the check box is unchecked. Now you add the code for the remaining CheckBox controls. Write the line of code needed for each remaining CheckBox in the following space:

_____

_____

_____

_____

### Step 5: Save Your Project

Save your project changes by clicking the **Save** button on the toolbar.

### Step 6: Run Your Program

The program should run exactly as it did in Project 4-1. The only difference is that the check boxes now work as the user expects. When a box is checked, that property is applied to the text. When it is unchecked, the property is taken away, all through the use of the If/Else structure.

One thing to keep in mind regarding both the If and If/Else structures is that each If or If/Else is tested, regardless of whether any of the conditions are met. That means that each condition test is independent of the other, which is demonstrated with Project 4-2.

A **radio button**, technically known as an **option button** in VB, allows the user to make one—and only one—choice. That means that the user can choose only one button on the *entire* form unless a **Frame** is used to gather groups of option buttons together. But the user can then choose only one option button from each group.

You will be modifying an existing project to allow it to take advantage of both the OptionButton control and the If/ElseIf structure. The If/ElseIf structure allows you to provide the perfect companion code to this type of control. If the one button is not selected, then it must be another. However, in this instance not every condition is tested. Once a matching condition is found, the If/ElseIf structure is exited, and the program moves on.

### Step 1: Start Your Compiler

Start your compiler, if necessary.

### Step 2: Open Project 3-2

Open the **File** menu and click **Open Project**. From the **Existing** tab in the Open Project dialog box, open your **Project 3-2** project. Your VB environment should look like Figure 4-7.

**FIGURE 4-7**
Project 3-2

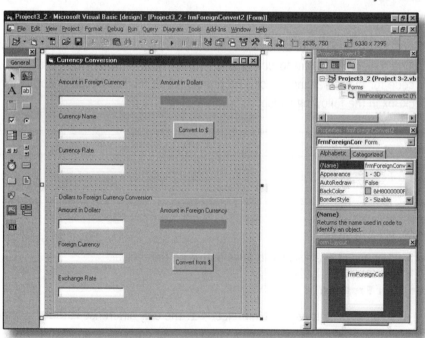

Save your form as **FCtoDoll** and your project as **Project 4-3**.

## Step 3: Modify Your Project

The first thing you need to do is move the Dollar To Foreign Currency controls to a separate form, leaving the Foreign Currency To Dollar controls on the FCtoDoll form. In order to do that, you must first add a new form to your project. Once you add the new form, you can then cut and paste or copy and paste your existing controls to the new form.

Be careful when copying the controls to the new form. Some of the label controls may not transfer because they were added to the frame control and not the form. If the labels do not come over, simply return to the first form and copy them one at a time. You may remove the frame control to make this project slightly easier.

The properties associated with each copied control will copy with the control. The code you added to your command buttons will also not transfer with the copy. The code is part of the form itself. You will need to cut and paste the code and the associated variable to the new form associated with the proper object and related procedure.

Once you have the controls on the proper forms and the code in the proper place, save your project.

## Step 5: Save Your Project

Save your project changes by clicking the **Save** button on the toolbar. The Save File As dialog box will open and prompt you to save your new form. Your default file name is Form1. Save your file as **DolltoFC**. The existing form and project are automatically saved.

Your forms should look similar to Figure 4-8 and Figure 4-9.

**FIGURE 4-8**
Project 4-3 FCtoDoll form

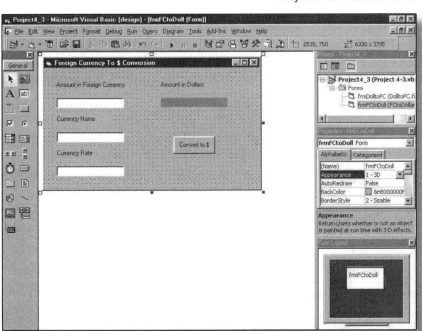

**FIGURE 4-9**
Project 4-3 DolltoFC form

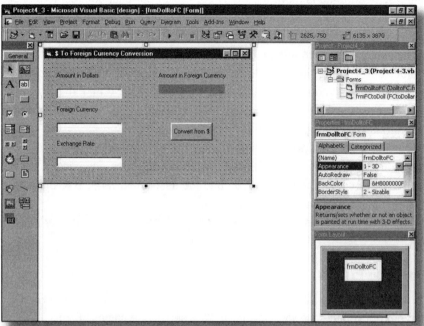

## Step 6: Add Your Main Form

Now you will add the form that will contain the option buttons. This program will enable users to choose which currency conversion they wish to perform. Does a user want to convert from a foreign currency into dollars or from dollars into a foreign currency? Your program will allow the user to make the choice.

One of your command buttons will execute the option button choice that the user makes, and the other will exit the program.

**1.** Add your new form to the project. Write down the name you will give to your main form. Make your choice meaningful.

_____

**2.** Change the Caption property of your new form. Write down the Caption you chose. Make your choice meaningful.

_____

**3.** Add one Label control, two OptionButton controls, and two Command button controls to your form. Write down the values you give to each property listed in the following chart.

| Control | Property | Value |
|---------|----------|-------|
| Label1 | Name | _____ |
| | Caption | _____ |
| Option1 | Name | _____ |
| | Caption | _____ |
| Option2 | Name | _____ |
| | Caption | _____ |

| Command1 | Name | _____ |
| | Caption | _____ |
| Command2 | Name | _____ |
| | Caption | _____ |

Position the forms so that they open on top of each other. Your form should look similar to the example in Figure 4-10.

FIGURE 4-10
Project 4-3 new form

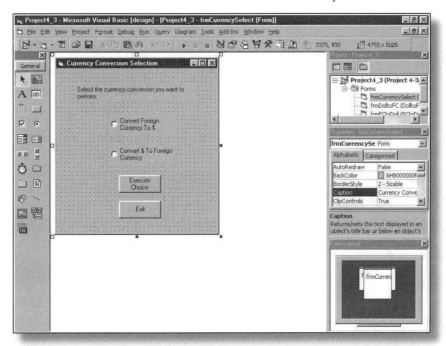

### Step 7: Save Your Project

Save your project changes by clicking the **Save** button on the toolbar. The Save File As dialog box will open and prompt you to save your new form. Your default file name is Form1. Save your file as the name you chose in Step 6. Do not include the frm prefix when you save the file. The existing forms and project are automatically saved.

### Step 8: Add Your Code to Your Option Buttons

You now need to add code to your command buttons. If the first option button is selected, it will enable the user to execute the Foreign Currency To Dollars form. If the second is selected, the Dollars To Foreign Currency form will be executed. You will also be using the If/ElseIf structure because only one option button can be selected at a time.

You will need to double-click each command button in order to enter the necessary code for each event. The Form window editing area will open to display the code attached to each command button. Figure 4-11 shows where each line of the code should be entered for each command button.

**FIGURE 4-11**

Code to be attached to each command button

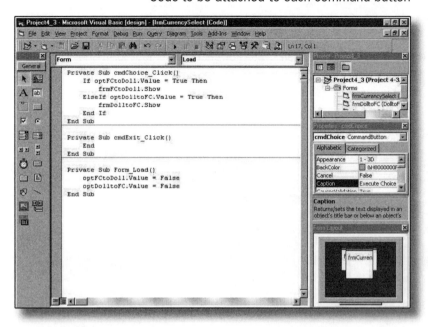

Again save your project after typing in this line of code. Now you can run your program.

### Step 9: Run the Program

Click the **Run** button on the toolbar to run the program. Your program should open in the middle of the screen. If your main form is not the first form to open, then you need to change the project properties to make it the first form to execute. (*Hint:* The project properties option is located on the Project submenu.)

Select which currency conversion you would like to run by clicking the option button and then clicking the **Execute Choice** command button. Both conversions should execute and return control to your main form when closed. The Exit button should exit the program. (*Hint:* You may need to change the TabIndex order of the controls on the DolltoFC form.)

### Step 10: Review Your Code

Now that your program has run successfully, answer the following questions. Review your answers with your classmates and teacher.

**1.** Explain the difference between a check box and an option button.

_____

_____

**2.** Explain the function of the If/ElseIf structure.

_____

_____

_____

**3.** Explain the purpose of your main form.

_____

_____

**4.** Explain the following block of code:

```
Private Sub Form_Load()
    optFCtoDoll.Value = False
    optDolltoFC.Value = False
End Sub
```

_____

_____

**5.** Explain the following block of code:

```
Private Sub cmdChoice_Click()
    If optFCtoDoll.Value = True Then
        frmFCtoDoll.Show
    ElseIf optDolltoFC.Value = True Then
        frmDolltoFC.Show
    End If
End Sub
```

_____

_____

**6.** Explain why you used an Exit command button when the user can exit the program by clicking on the Close (X) button in the upper right corner of the window.

_____

_____

**7.** Explain the overall execution of the program.

_____

_____

_____

_____

You have now used a few new controls and multiple If structures to add control to your programs.

## PROJECT 4 - 4 : The Select Case Structure Ⓑ

The last selection control structure you will use is the Select Case structure. The Select Case structure lends itself to checking for multiple conditions. This structure helps alleviate the mess that can be caused by using multiple embedded If/Else statements.

In this project you will create a program that will convert percentage grades into letter grades. You can use your own school's grading scale in place of the one presented here. Your program will allow the user to input a numeric grade and then have it converted to a letter grade.

**Step 1: Start Your Compiler**

Start your compiler if it is not already running.

**Step 2: Create a New Project**

Open the **File** menu and click **New Project**. In the New Project window, double-click the **Standard EXE** button. The Project1 file opens, displaying a blank form named Form1.

**Step 3: Add Your Controls**

For this project you will need three Label controls, one Command Button control, and one TextBox control. Resize your form and place your controls as shown in Figure 4-12.

Copying/scanning is not permitted and may be a violation of copyright laws.
© 2000 by South-Western Educational Publishing.

**FIGURE 4-12**
Changing the size of the form and adding controls

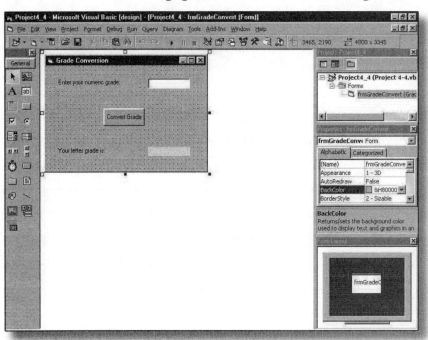

Change the appropriate properties for each control as outlined in the following chart:

| Control | Property | Value |
| --- | --- | --- |
| Project | Name | Project4_4 |
| Form | Name | frmGradeConvert |
|  | Caption | Grade Conversion |
| Text1 | Name | txtNumeric |
|  | Alignment | Right Justify |
|  | Text | None |

| Command1 | Name | cmdConvert |
|---|---|---|
| | Caption | Convert Grade |
| Label1 | Name | lblEnter |
| | Caption | Enter your numeric grade: |
| Label2 | Name | lblLetter |
| | Caption | Your letter grade is: |
| Label3 | Name | lblGrade |
| | Alignment | Right Justify |
| | BackColor | &H0080FFFF& (Light Yellow) |
| | Caption | None |

**Step 4: Save Your Project**

Save your form as **GradeConvert** and your project as **Project 4-4**.

**Step 5: Add Your Code to the Project**

Now that your form and project have been designed, it is time to add the necessary code to the controls. With this project you will add code to the Command Button control.

Double-click the **Command Button** control and modify the existing line of code between the "Private Sub" and "End Sub" lines of code to read as shown in the following gray box. This is the format used for the Select Case structure.

```
Private Sub cmdConvert_Click()
    Select Case txtNumeric.Text
        Case Is >= 93
            lblGrade.Caption = "A"
        Case Is >= 85
            lblGrade.Caption = "B"
        Case Is >= 77
            lblGrade.Caption = "C"
        Case Is >= 70
            lblGrade.Caption = "D"
        Case Else
            lblGrade.Caption = "F"
    End Select
End Sub
```

Make sure you save both the form and the project again by clicking the **Save** button on the toolbar.

These lines of code perform as follows. The Select Case line reads the value entered into the text box by the user. The value is then compared to each Case line. When a match occurs, the line of code embedded within that Case is performed. The Case Else performs only if no other Case results in a match.

**Step 6: Run the Program**

Click the **Run** button on the toolbar to run your program. Your program should open in the middle of the screen. Type a numeric grade into the text box and then click the **Convert Grade** button. The numeric grade you entered is then converted into a letter grade. You can make the program specific to your school by modifying the code to reflect the grade scale in place at your school.

### Step 7: Review Your Code

Now that your program has run successfully (at least somewhat), answer the following questions. Review your answers with your classmates and teacher.

**1.** Explain the reason behind using a Select Case structure versus an If/Else structure.

_____

_____

_____

**2.** Explain the Case Else comparison.

_____

_____

**3.** Explain the overall execution of the program.

_____

_____

You have now created programs that use all the selection control structures.

## PROJECT 4 - 5 : Simple Repetitions   (B)

In this project you will use all the repetition structures on the same form. Each repetition structure will produce the same results; however, they will each use different code. You will see how each structure compares with the other.

### Step 1: Start Your Compiler

Start your compiler if it is not already running.

### Step 2: Create a New Project

Open the **File** menu and click **New Project**. In the New Project window, double-click the **Standard EXE** button. The Project1 file opens, displaying a blank form named Form1.

### Step 3: Add Your Controls

For this project you will need six Command Button controls. Resize your form and place your controls as shown in Figure 4-13.

**FIGURE 4-13**
Changing the size of the form and adding controls

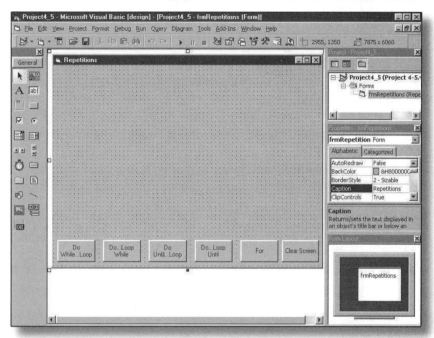

Change the appropriate properties for each control as outlined in the following chart:

| Control | Property | Value |
|---|---|---|
| Project | Name | Project4_5 |
| Form | Name | frmRepetitions |
| | Caption | Repetitions |
| | Font | Webdings Regular 14 |
| Command1 | Name | cmdDoWhile |
| | Caption | Do While...Loop |
| Command2 | Name | cmdLoopWhile |
| | Caption | Do...Loop While |
| Command3 | Name | cmdDoUntil |
| | Caption | Do Until...Loop |
| Command4 | Name | cmdLoopUntil |
| | Caption | Do...Loop Until |
| Command5 | Name | cmdFor |
| | Caption | For |
| Command6 | Name | cmdClear |
| | Caption | Clear Screen |

### Step 4: Save Your Project

Open the **File** menu and click **Save Project As**. In the Save File As dialog box, change the default file name to **Repetitions**. Select the folder and/or disk containing your course files. Then click the **Save** button.

Once the form file is saved, the Save Project As window opens. Make sure you are saving to the same course folder. Then rename the project to **Project 4-5**. Click the **Save** button. Once the project is saved, the information displayed in the Project window should look the same as in Figure 4-13.

### Step 5: Add Your Code to the Project

You will be adding code to each of the six Command Button controls in order to display the word "Hello" on the form using the Webdings font. To make sure that each repetition structure performs properly, each time the word displays, it will be in a slightly different position. You will use **X, Y coordinates** to place the word.

The bulk of the code under each Command Button control will be identical. However, the structure that encases the code will differ. You will also use the **FormLoad** procedure to set the form display measurements.

First, double-click any **Command Button** control. When the code editing window opens, select the **Form** object from the Object list box. Then add the following code between the "Private Sub" and "End Sub" lines.

```
Private Sub Form_Load()
    frmRepetitions.ScaleMode = vbTwips
End Sub
```

This allows you to use **twips** as your form of measurement when moving your word around the form. A twip is 1/1440 of an inch or 1/567 of a centimeter. VB also provides you with the option of using points, characters, inches, or centimeters as the form of measurement.

Make sure you save your project again by clicking the **Save** button on the toolbar.

Next you will add code to your "Do While...Loop" command button. Double-click on the button to open the code editing window. Then enter the following block of code between the "Private Sub" and "End Sub" lines.

```
Private Sub cmdDoWhile_Click()
    Dim intCounter As Integer
    Dim intXPos As Integer
    Dim intYPos As Integer

    CurrentX = 0
    CurrentY = 0
    intCounter = 1

    Do While intCounter <= 10
        intXPos = frmRepetitions.CurrentX
        intYPos = frmRepetitions.CurrentY
        frmRepetitions.Print "Hello"
        frmRepetitions.CurrentX = intXPos + 150
        frmRepetitions.CurrentY = intYPos + 200
        intCounter = intCounter + 1
    Loop
End Sub
```

The majority of this block of code will be used for each command button with the exception of the Clear Screen button.

The three variables declared are for the counter you will use for your repetitions and the *X, Y* form coordinates. Each variable is then ***initialized***. All three of these variables will be ***local*** to each procedure because you declare them within the procedure. The set of three variables is not the same when switching from procedure to procedure. Even though they are named the same, they are different because each set belongs to a different procedure.

After you declare and then initialize the variables, you then code the loop. This first procedure uses the ***Do While...Loop*** structure. The format is as follows:

```
Do While (the condition is so)
      Perform a block of code
Loop
```

The condition is tested immediately. Because of this, the loop may never perform. While the condition is met, the block of code is performed. It then loops until the condition is not met. All loops perform in a similar manner.

The first two lines within the loop assign the current *X, Y* print positions of the form to your intXPos and intYPos variables. This will allow you to change the print position on the form. The third line prints the word *Hello* using the Webdings font. Remember, you assigned the Webdings font using the form's font property. The next two lines reposition the *X, Y* coordinates for the next time the word *Hello* is printed on the form. Then the last line increases your counter by one. The loop sends you back to the top to determine whether the condition is still true. If so, you loop again. If not, the procedure ends.

You will be introduced to the other loop structures, and then you will be required to code the other four loop control buttons.

The ***Do...Loop While*** structure works in basically the same manner. The difference is that the condition is tested at the end of the structure. This way the loop will be performed at least one time. The structure is outlined as follows:

```
Do
      Perform a block of code
Loop While (the condition is so)
```

The ***Do Until...Loop*** structure is one that will perform until a condition is met. Instead of the loop occurring while the condition is being met, this loop occurs because the condition has not been met. Because the condition test occurs at the beginning of the loop, the loop may never perform. The structure is outlined as follows:

```
Do Until (the condition is so)
      Perform a block of code
Loop
```

The ***Do...Loop Until*** structure matches with the Do...Loop While structure. The condition is tested at the end, which ensures that the loop will perform at least one time. Otherwise, the logic is the same as the Do...Until Loop—loop until the condition is met. The structure is outlined as follows:

```
Do
      Perform a block of code
Loop Until (the condition is so)
```

**8 3**

The last of the repetition structures is the For structure. The **For** structure sets up a counter that counts through the loops for you. The For loop is performed until the limit plus 1 is reached. When the counter is more than the upper limit of the loop, the loop terminates. While the For loop has not reached the upper limit, the block of code contained within the For structure is performed. The Next statement tells the For loop to continue. The For structure was outlined for you in the Introduction, and we will show you again here:

```
For counter = 1 To 10 Step 1
        Perform a block of code
Next
```

Now it is your turn to code the remaining loop Command Button controls. Using the Do While...Loop as the basis, write your code for each remaining button in the following space:

Do...Loop While

_____

_____

_____

_____

_____

_____

_____

_____

_____

_____

_____

_____

_____

_____

_____

_____

_____

Do Until...Loop

_____

_____

_____

_____

_____

_____

_____

_____

_____

_____

_____

_____

_____

_____

Do…Loop Until

_____

_____

_____

_____

_____

_____

_____

_____

_____

_____

_____

_____

For

_____

_____

_____

_____

_____

_____

_____

_____

_____

_____

_____

_____

_____

_____

_____

_____

The last command button is simple. All it does is remove the printing from the form so that you can tell that each button actually works. Double-click the **Clear Screen** button to open the code editing window. Type the following line of code in the proper place:

```
Private Sub cmdClear_Click()

    frmRepetitions.Refresh

End Sub
```

All of your Command Button controls should be properly coded.

### Step 6: Run the Program

Click the **Run** button on the toolbar to run your program. Your program should open in the middle of the screen. Click each command button to test that it works. Click the **Clear Screen** button to erase the printing between using the different command buttons. The same thing should appear on the screen for each button. The reason is that you used the same code for each button. Feel free to change the body of the code in any way you like after your teacher reviews this project.

### Step 7: Review Your Code

Now that your program has run successfully, answer the following questions. Review your answers with your classmates and teacher.

**1.** Explain the logic behind the Do While…Loop structure.

_____

_____

**2.** Explain the logic behind the Do…Loop While structure.

_____

_____

**3.** Explain the logic behind the Do Until…Loop structure.

_____

_____

**8 6**

**4.** Explain the logic behind the Do...Loop Until structure.

_____

_____

**5.** Explain the logic behind the For loop.

_____

_____

_____

**6.** Explain the following line of code:

```
frmRepetitions.Refresh
```

_____

**7.** If your code remained consistent between each repetition structure in this project, there will be a slight difference in the output between the Do While loops and the Do Until loops. What is the difference, and why does it occur?

_____

_____

You have now created a program that uses all the repetition control structures.

## P R O J E C T  4 - 6 :  Compound Interest    Ⓑ

**SCANS**

In this project you will use the For repetition structure to create a program that will calculate the compound interest on an investment. If you were to put so much money away for so many years at a given interest rate, how much would you have at the end of that time? Given the problems with Social Security, this should be a question in which you are very interested!

You will provide users with control over the amount they invest, the time period for which they will invest, and the interest rate their money will earn. Then your program will calculate the balance they will have at the end of their investment period.

### Step 1: Start Your Compiler

Start your compiler if it is not already running.

### Step 2: Create a New Project

Open the **File** menu and click **New Project**. In the New Project window, double-click the **Standard EXE** button. The Project1 file opens, displaying a blank form named Form1.

### Step 3: Add Your Controls

For this project you will need five Labels, three TextBox controls, and one Command Button control. Resize your form and place your controls as shown in Figure 4-14.

**FIGURE 4-14**

Changing the size of the form and adding controls

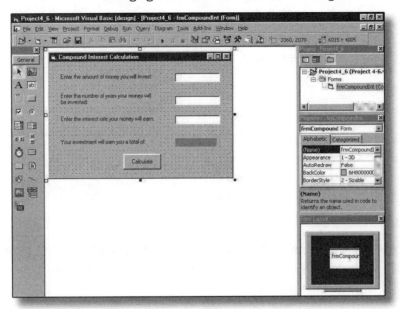

Change the appropriate properties for each control as outlined below.

| Control | Property | Value |
|---|---|---|
| Project | Name | Project4_6 |
| Form | Name | frmCompoundInt |
| | Caption | Compound Interest Calculation |
| Command1 | Name | cmdCalculate |
| | Caption | Calculate |
| | TabIndex | 4 |
| Label1 | Name | lblPrin |
| | Caption | Enter the amount of money you will invest: |
| Label2 | Name | lblYears |
| | Caption | Enter the number of years your money will be invested: |
| Label3 | Name | lblInt |
| | Caption | Enter the interest rate your money will earn: |
| Label4 | Name | lblResponse |
| | Caption | Your investment will earn you a total of: |
| Label5 | Name | lblAnswer |
| | Alignment | Right Justify |
| | BackColor | &H0000FF00& (Green) |
| | Caption | None |
| Text1 | Name | txtPrin |
| | Alignment | Right Justify |
| | TabIndex | 1 |
| | Text | None |

| | | |
|---|---|---|
| Text2 | Name | txtYears |
| | Alignment | Right Justify |
| | TabIndex | 2 |
| | Text | None |
| Text3 | Name | txtInt |
| | Alignment | Right Justify |
| | TabIndex | 3 |
| | Text | None |

### Step 4: Save Your Project

Open the **File** menu and click **Save Project As**. In the Save File As dialog box, change the default file name to **CompoundInt**. Select the folder and/or disk containing your course files. Then click the **Save** button.

Once the form file is saved, the Save Project As window opens. Make sure you are saving to the same course folder. Then rename the project to **Project 4-6**. Click the **Save** button. Once the project is saved, the information displayed in the Project window should look the same as in Figure 4-14.

### Step 5: Add Your Code to the Project

You will be adding code to your only Command Button control, plus you will need to initialize a few variables. Double-click the **Command Button** control to open the code editing window.

Type the following blocks of code in the proper places:

```
Dim intCounter As Integer
Dim curAnswer As Currency
Dim intPeriods As Integer
Dim curPerPeriod As Currency
```

```
Private Sub cmdCalculate_Click()
    intPeriods = Val(txtYears.Text) * 12
    curPerPeriod = Val(txtInt.Text) / 100 / 12
    curAnswer = Val(txtPrin.Text)

    For intCounter = 1 To intPeriods
        curAnswer = curAnswer + (curAnswer * curPerPeriod)
    Next

    lblAnswer.Caption = Format(curAnswer, "Currency")
End Sub
```

Your Command Button controls should be properly coded.

### Step 6: Run the Program

Click the **Run** button on the toolbar to run your program. Your program should open in the middle of the screen. Enter an amount in each of the text boxes and then click the **Calculate** button. You will receive an answer in currency format.

### Step 7: Review Your Code

Now that your program has run successfully, answer the following questions. Review your answers with your classmates and teacher.

**8 9**

**1.** Where did you place the following block of code? Explain why.

```
Dim intCounter As Integer
Dim curAnswer As Currency
Dim intPeriods As Integer
Dim curPerPeriod As Currency
```

_____

_____

_____

**2.** Explain why curAnswer was declared as a currency type instead of a decimal type.

_____

_____

**3.** Explain each of the following lines of code:

```
intPeriods = Val(txtYears.Text) * 12
curPerPeriod = Val(txtInt.Text) / 100 / 12
curAnswer = Val(txtPrin.Text)
```

_____

_____

_____

**4.** Explain the following For structure:

```
For intCounter = 1 To intPeriods
    curAnswer = curAnswer + (curAnswer * curPerPeriod)
Next
```

_____

_____

_____

**5.** Explain the following line of code:

```
lblAnswer.Caption = Format(curAnswer, "Currency")
```

**6.** Explain the overall execution of the program.

_____

_____

_____

_____

You have now created a program that will help you plan for retirement.

# *Summary*

This lesson reviewed every control structure in Visual Basic. You began by reviewing the fact that VB does not lend itself to sequential control unless you are referring to the code attached to each specific control. There is no overall code sequence as in other languages. However, the other control structures remain viable.

You then coded a number of programs that familiarized you with selection structures. You created programs using If, If/Else, If/ElseIf structures and related controls, such as OptionButtons and Check-Boxes. You changed font properties, created menu type choices, and converted numeric grades into letter grades using the techniques provided in this lesson.

The last two projects focused your attention on repetition structures. VB provides the Do While...Loop, the Do...Loop While, the Do Until...Loop, the Do...Loop Until, and the For repetition structures. You coded programs using every repetition structure, otherwise known as loops.

## LESSON 4 REVIEW QUESTIONS

### SHORT ANSWER

**Define the following in the space provided.**

1. Sequence control structure

_____

_____

2. Selection control structure

_____

3. Repetition control structure

_____

4. Top-down programming

_____

_____

5. Modules

_____

6. Procedures

_____

7. Decision making

_____

_____

**8.** If structure

_____

**9.** If/Else structure

_____

_____

**10.** If/ElseIf structure

_____

_____

**11.** Looping

_____

**12.** Endless loop

_____

**13.** Do While structure

_____

**14.** Do Until structure

_____

**15.** For structure

_____

**16.** Counter

_____

**17.** Increment

_____

_____

**18.** Step

_____

**19.** Default value

_____

**20.** CheckBox

_____

**21.** Prefix

_____

_____

**22.** Font property

_____

_____

**23.** Ellipsis

_____

_____

**24.** Condition

_____

**25.** FontBold

_____

_____

**26.** Compile error

_____

**27.** Radio button

_____

_____

**28.** OptionButton

_____

**29.** Frame control

_____

_____

**30.** *X, Y* coordinates

_____

**31.** FormLoad procedure

_____

**32.** Twips

_____

_____

**33.** Local

_____

_____

**34.** Initialized

_____

**35.** Currency format

_____

**36.** Format

_____

## WRITTEN QUESTIONS

**Write your answers to the following questions in the space provided.**

**1.** Explain why Visual Basic does not have a true sequence control structure.

_____

_____

_____

**2.** Explain the differences between the If, If/Else, and the If/ElseIf selection structures.

_____

_____

_____

_____

_____

_____

_____

_____

**3.** Explain the Select Case structure.

_____

_____

_____

**4.** List all of the repetition control structures and explain the differences between them.

_____

_____

_____

_____

_____

_____

_____

_____

_____

_____

_____

**5.** Explain the difference between the use of a CheckBox control and an OptionButton control.

_____

_____

**6.** Explain how it is possible to allow the user to select more than one option button on a form.

_____

_____

**7.** Explain how to add labels to a frame.

_____

**8.** Explain how to "print" to a form.

_____

_____

**9.** Define and explain a twip.

_____

_____

## TESTING YOUR SKILLS

 **Estimated Time:**

Application 4-1  1 ¹/₂ hours
Application 4-2  1 hour

### APPLICATION 4-1

In Project 3-5 you created a simple menu form that allowed the user to select from a variety of calculation programs. The user could make a selection by clicking on the command button related to that menu choice.

In this application you will create a new project that uses option buttons for the menu form. The same calculation form from Project 3-5 will be called when the appropriate option button is selected.

**1.** Open a new project.

**2.** Use the default form to create a menu form similar to the one in Project 3-5. This time use option buttons instead of command buttons to allow the user to make a choice.

**3.** Add any other necessary controls. You may want to add a Command Button control to control the option button selections.

**4.** Add any necessary code to the appropriate controls.

5. Add the remaining forms from Project 3-5 to this new project.

6. Save your project. Use **OptionMenu** as the form name and **App4-1** as the project name. You can use the same form names for the other forms. In order to differentiate them from the forms from Project 3-5 you may want to add a number to the form name. If you save your forms with different names, remember to change the form names within the project.

7. Run your project to test it. Then debug it if necessary. Run it again.

## APPLICATION 4-2

In this application you will add three check boxes to your Project 4-2. The three CheckBox controls will add colors to your font conversion.

1. Open your **Project 4-2**. Save the form as **FontConvertApp**, and then save your project as **App4-2**.

2. Rename your project and form within the project to match the new filenames.

3. Modify the form so that it contains six CheckBox controls—the original three and three additional for the colors. One color will be red, the next green, and the last blue.

4. Change the properties for each new CheckBox control. Then add the appropriate code to the new CheckBoxes.

5. Save your project.

6. Run your project to test it. Then debug it if necessary. Run it again. Do not code the command buttons.

## CRITICAL THINKING

 **Estimated Time: 6 hours**

Create a payroll calculation program.

First, create a menu form that will allow the user to choose from different features. For example, one choice could be entering daily hours, another calculating total hours for the week, and another calculating paychecks.

Second, create programs for each menu selection that will allow the user to actually perform the functions they have chosen to perform. Use selection and repetition structures where appropriate. For example, when entering hours, use OptionButton controls to allow the user to choose for which days they are entering hours. When calculating payroll, you may use OptionButton controls within Frames to allow the user to choose between Marital Status for Income Tax and Medical Benefit calculations.

Then, using the Format function, begin to format your output displays. Add any additional forms and procedures you would like.

# MENUS, DIALOG BOX CONTROLS, AND MOUSE EVENTS

## OBJECTIVES

**Upon completion of this lesson, you should be able to:**

■ Demonstrate the use of the Menu Editor.

■ Design menus and submenus for programs.

■ Set up accelerator keys and checked menu options.

■ Implement common dialog box controls.

■ Differentiate between the various mouse events.

■ Illustrate the use of the different mouse events.

🕑 **Estimated Time: 8 hours**

## *Introduction*

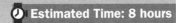

$T$his lesson presents you with a variety of tools that can further spruce up and add control to your programs. You begin by adding *menus* and *submenus* to existing programs. Almost all Visual Basic programs provide a *menu bar* of some type to add convenience. *Every* Windows program should work with or without a mouse—some users like using the keyboard more than the mouse, and the mouse may not function properly. You also learn about *accelerator keys*, which speed keyboard access, and *checked menu options*, which are the menu equivalent of option buttons.

You are then introduced to the *Common Dialog Box* control, which actually represents six different dialog boxes. The reason that the control is called the *common* dialog box is that users have come to expect their dialog boxes to behave in a similar manner. And users should get what they expect! In this lesson you are introduced to the *font selection* dialog boxes. From there you explore *mouse events*. You have already been exposed to the most obvious mouse event—the *click*. Almost every program has something happen when the mouse is clicked on a control, usually a command button. In this lesson you experiment with the *double-click*, *right-click*, *drag-and-drop operation*, and the typical *click*.

This lesson focuses on the following:

■ **Demonstrating the Menu Editor.** The Menu Editor is not part of the VB Toolbox. You will learn where to find it and how to use it to create menus for your applications.

■ **Designing menus and submenus for programs and setting up accelerator keys and checked menu options.** You will program your menus to be more responsive to users' needs. Your menus should be organized similar to what users see in other applications and should provide keyboard shortcuts.

**9 7**

- **Implementing common dialog box controls.** Common dialog box controls provide users with control over choices while allowing you to maintain program control. You will use two of the six boxes in this lesson.

- **Differentiating between and illustrating the use of the various mouse events.** So far you have worked with the most obvious mouse event, which is the single click. In this lesson you experiment with four other mouse events.

## PROJECT 5-1 : Menus (B)

The Toolbox in Visual Basic does not contain menu creation tools. In order to begin creating a menu, you must use the Menu Editor, which can be found on the Tools menu. You will be using the Menu Editor to create menus, submenus, accelerator keys, and checked menu options.

In this project you will modify the font conversion application you last modified in Application 4-2. The basic idea of this program is to create a useful menu for the users of your application. You will be adding all the necessary controls to this application.

### Step 1: Start Your Compiler

Start your compiler if it is not already running.

### Step 2: Open App4-2

Open the **File** menu and click **Open Project**. From the Existing tab in the Open Project dialog box, open your **App4-2** project. Your VB environment should look like Figure 5-1.

**FIGURE 5-1**
App4-2 project

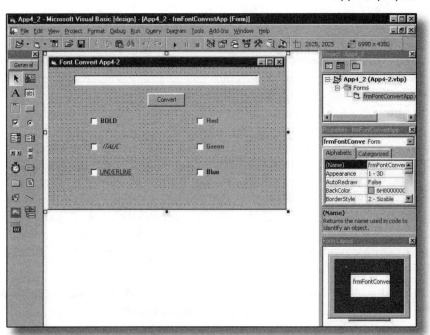

Save your form as **FontConvertMenu** and your project as **Project 5-1**.

**9 8**

## Step 3: Create Your Menu

Your form will not need to be changed. All the existing controls will remain as they are. The code that you have already added to your controls may prove to be useful in coding your menu.

Open the **Menu Editor** by selecting it on the **Tools** menu. If the Menu Editor option is grayed out, click on your form and try to select it again. The Menu Editor should look like Figure 5-2. The Menu Editor takes the place of the Properties window used for your other controls. The top half of the Menu Editor is where you will set the ***Menu properties*** for each menu option. The bottom half is the ***Menu control list box***, which displays a hierarchical view of your menu.

**FIGURE 5-2**
Menu Editor

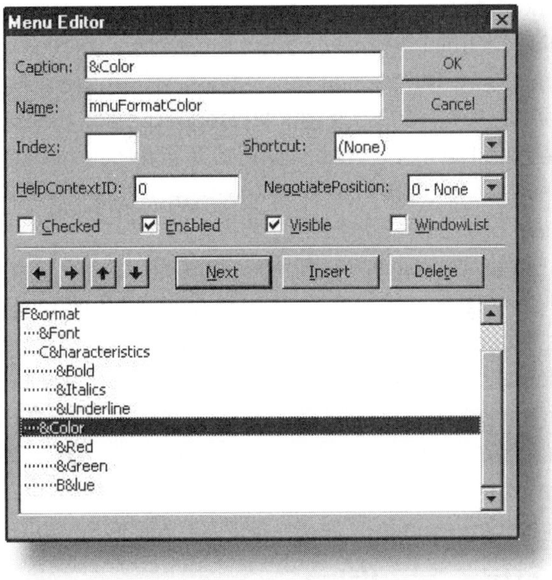

You will be working within the Menu Editor until you begin adding code to your menu options. You will be creating 12 menu options for your menu. The two main properties you will be using for this project are the ***Caption*** and ***Name*** properties. You will also be using the ***Enabled*** and ***Visible*** properties; however, these two are selected by default.

The Caption property is the label that will appear on your menu. The Name property is how you will refer to the menu option in your code. The Enabled property means that the menu option is active, and the Visible property means that the user can see the option.

When you create a menu option, you will also designate its accelerator key, which is the keyboard combination that will execute that specific menu option. The accelerator key is the key letter that is preceded by an ampersand (&).

Your menu bar will contain two main menus: File and Format. The File menu will contain one option: Exit. The Format menu will contain three options: Font, Characteristics, and Color. The Characteristics and Color options will each have a submenu level. The Characteristics option will have a submenu that consists of the Bold, Italics, and Underline options. The Color option will have a submenu that contains the Red, Green, and Blue options. The Menu control list box in Figure 5-2 provides a view of this menu layout.

**HOT TIP**

Avoid having more than two submenu levels because it will be confusing to users.

The first menu we will create is the File menu. Enter the following information in the appropriate text box:

| Option | Property | Value |
|--------|----------|-------|
| File | Caption | &File |
|  | Name | mnuFile |

Leave both the **Enabled** and **Visible** properties checked. All of your menu options will be both Enabled and Visible. Your File menu properties should look like Figure 5-2.

The **ampersand** in front of the "F" in the Caption text box designates that key as the accelerator key. The Alt key pressed in combination with the accelerator key opens that menu. Once you open the menu, you simply need to press the accelerator key shown for the submenu option.

Each menu option must have a unique name. Even though the options are created using the Menu Editor, they are still controls, and all controls must have unique names. All menu options should begin with the mnu prefix. The naming conventions will expand as we move into submenus.

Click **OK** to close the Menu Editor. Save your project by clicking the **Save** button, and then run your program. You will see the File menu option appear on your new menu bar. The letter "F" is underlined because you have designated it as your accelerator key. The File option will not do anything yet because you have not added code.

Reopen your Menu Editor. You will now add additional options to your menu.

The &File option will be highlighted in the menu control list box. Click the **Next** button, which is located just above the list box. The highlight in the list box will drop down one line, and the menu properties part of the Menu Editor should be empty except for the defaults. You will now create the Exit option on your File menu.

Click the right-pointing arrow key above the list box. You will see an **ellipsis** ( **. . .** ) appear in the list box. This designates that the Exit option will be part of the File menu. Type in the following information in the menu properties area.

| Option | Property | Value |
|--------|----------|-------|
| Exit | Caption | E&xit |
|  | Name | mnuFileExit |

Leave the **Enabled** and **Visible** properties checked for all of your menu options.

Notice that the naming convention has changed for the menu option. The name of the Exit option is mnuFileExit. The *mnu* designates it as a menu option; the *File* designates that it belongs to the File menu option; and the *Exit* is the name of this option. This may be rather long, but the name indicates where it will appear on your menu.

Now you will create the Format menu. Click the **Next** button. The highlight will drop down one line with the ellipsis automatically inserted. Since the Format menu will be equal to the File menu, you do *not* want it to be indented. Click the left-pointing arrow to delete the ellipsis. Enter the following values for the menu properties:

| Option | Property | Value |
|--------|----------|-------|
| Format | Caption | F&ormat |
|  | Name | mnuFormat |

The remainder of the menu options will be the Format menu's submenus. Click the **Next** button, and then click the right-pointing arrow. You should be one line below the Format option in the list box, and an ellipsis should be inserted. Enter the following values for the three menu options. After adding the first option, you will need to click the **Next** button to drop to the next line.

| Option | Property | Value |
|---|---|---|
| Font | Caption | &Font |
| | Name | mnuFormatFont |
| Characteristics | Caption | C&haracteristics |
| | Name | mnuFormatChar |
| Color | Caption | &Color |
| | Name | mnuFormatColor |

Now you will create the Characteristics and Color submenus. You will need to backtrack slightly to insert these menu options.

Select the **Color** option, and click the **Insert** button, which is located above the menu control list box. A line is inserted just above the Color option. The inserted line contains the same indentation that the Color line contains. This would allow you to place your next menu option at the same level as the Characteristic option. However, this line will be a submenu for the Characteristics option. Therefore, you need to indent one additional level. Do this by clicking the right-pointing arrow. Another ellipsis is added to the existing ellipsis. You are now one level under the Characteristic option.

Add the following Characteristic submenu options:

| Option | Property | Value |
|---|---|---|
| Bold | Caption | &Bold |
| | Name | mnuFormatCharBold |
| Italics | Caption | &Italics |
| | Name | mnuFormatCharItalics |
| Underline | Caption | &Underline |
| | Name | mnuFormatCharUnder |

Notice the naming convention values. They tell you exactly where the option is on your menu.

Notice also that some of your accelerator keys have been repeats. The accelerator keys on the submenus can be repeats of the accelerator keys used on other levels. However, they must be unique on their own level.

Now add the submenu options for the Color menu. The information you need is as follows:

| Option | Property | Value |
|---|---|---|
| Red | Caption | &Red |
| | Name | mnuFormatColorRed |
| Green | Caption | &Green |
| | Name | mnuFormatColorGreen |
| Blue | Caption | &Blue |
| | Name | mnuFormatColorBlue |

You now have a menu for this project. Before the menu is fully functional, you need to add code to the menu options.

**Step 4: Save Your Project**

Save your project changes by clicking the **Save** button on the toolbar.

**Step 5: Add Your Code to the Project**

Adding code to menu options is as easy as adding code to any other control. With your form open in the Form editing window, simply select the menu option to which you want to add code to and click it.

The easiest option to code first is the Exit option on the File menu. Click **File** on the form's menu bar, and then click **Exit** on the menu. Your code editing window will open with the ***wrapper lines*** displayed. The wrapper lines are the first and last lines required for an event. Type in the following line of code between the wrapper lines:

```
End
```

Make sure you save both the form and the project again by clicking the **Save** button on the toolbar.

You now need to test the Exit menu option. Run your program. When it starts, click **File** on your application's menu bar, and then click **Exit**. Your program should end.

You will now add code to the menu options that you will be using for this program. You will be coding the three Characteristics submenu options and the three Color submenu options. You will be shown the code for one of the Characteristics submenu options and one of the Color submenu options. Then you will code the others on your own.

Click the **Format** option on your menu bar, click the **Characteristics** submenu option, and then click the **Bold** option. Your code editing window will open. Enter the following block of code for the *mnuFormatCharBold_Click()* procedure.

```
Private Sub mnuFormatCharBold_Click()
    mnuFormatCharBold.Checked = True
    lblChanged.FontBold = True
    mnuFormatCharItalics.Checked = False
    lblChanged.FontItalic = False
    mnuFormatCharUnder.Checked = False
    lblChanged.FontUnderline = False
End Sub
```

This block of code will set the option's Checked property to "True." This means that a check mark will appear next to this option when it is selected by the user. The label, lblChanged, that displays the converted font will have its FontBold property set to "True." Whatever appears on the label will be displayed in bold. The other lines of code remove the possibility that any of the other two options will be checked and that the label will not display anything in italics or underlined.

This type of code makes the three submenu choices mutually exclusive. Only one characteristics can be applied at a time, unlike the CheckBoxes on the body of the form. These menu options are ***checked menu options***. Only one can be checked at a time.

Use the preceding block of code as a guide in coding the Italics and Underline submenu options.

**1.** Write the block of code needed for the Italics option in the following space:

_____

_____

**1 0 2**

_____

_____

_____

_____

_____

_____

**2.** Write the block of code needed for the Underline option in the following space:

_____

_____

_____

_____

_____

_____

_____

_____

Save your project and then test your menu options after completing a set. This way you can see if you are coding your menu options properly.

Now you will enter the code for the Red option on the Color submenu. You will be shown the code for this option, and then you will code the others on your own.

Click the **Format** option on your menu bar, click the **Color** option, and then click the **Red** option. Your code editing window will open. Enter the following block of code for the *mnuFormatColorRed_Click()* procedure:

```
Private Sub mnuFormatColorRed_Click()
    mnuFormatColorRed.Checked = True
    lblChanged.ForeColor = vbRed
    mnuFormatColorGreen.Checked = False
    mnuFormatColorBlue.Checked = False
End Sub
```

This block of code will set the option's Checked property to "True." This means that a check mark will appear next to this option when it is selected by the user. The label, lblChanged, that displays the converted font will have its ForeColor property set to "vbRed." Whatever appears on the label will be displayed in red. The other lines of code remove the possibility that either of the other two options will be checked.

The vbRed value assigned to lblChanged.ForeColor is a ***named constant***, which is a name VB applies to a set of internal values. In this case vbRed applies a set color value to the ForeColor property.

Use the preceding block of code as a guide in coding the Green and Blue submenu options.

**1.** Write the block of code needed for the Green option in the following space:

_____

_____

**1 0 3**

_____
_____
_____
_____

**2.** Write the block of code needed for the Blue option in the following space:

_____
_____
_____
_____
_____
_____

### Step 6: Run the Program

Click the **Run** button on the toolbar to run your program. Your program should open in the middle of the screen. Type a line of text into the text box. Select the various menu choices from your menu bar. Notice that the text you typed in the text box is now displayed on the label with the appropriate characteristics: bold, italic, and/or underlined, and/or the appropriate color: red, green, or blue. Also pay attention to the operation of the menu options. You can choose only one menu option at a time from each submenu. You cannot apply multiple characteristics as you can with your check boxes.

### Step 7: Review Your Code

Now that your program has run successfully, answer the following questions. Review your answers with your classmates and teacher.

**1.** Explain the purpose of a menu.

_____
_____
_____

**2.** Explain the naming convention used for menu options.

_____
_____

**3.** Explain the two parts of the Menu Editor.

_____
_____
_____

**4.** Explain the use of the Next key.

_____

_____

**5.** Explain the use of the Insert key.

_____

_____

**6.** Explain the use of the arrow keys.

_____

_____

**7.** Explain accelerator keys.

_____

_____

**8.** Explain how to trigger accelerator keys on the menu bar.

_____

**9.** Explain how to trigger accelerator keys on submenus.

_____

**10.** Explain why you must add code to menu options.

_____

_____

_____

You are able to add menus to your programs.

## P R O J E C T   5 - 2 : Dialog Box Controls   Ⓑ

In this project you will add a Common Dialog Box control to Project 5-1. The Font option, located on the Format menu, is where the control will be placed. This means that when you click the Font option, a Font dialog box will open from which the user can make selections regarding the font of text.

You will begin by adding the Microsoft Common Dialog Control 6.0, or the Microsoft Common Dialog Control 5.0 in Visual Basic 5.0, to your Toolbox and then adding the control to your form. This control can take the form of six different dialog boxes. In this project you will add the control, then change its properties, and add code so that it acts as the Font dialog box.

### Step 1: Start Your Compiler

Start your compiler if necessary.

## Step 2: Open Project 5-1

Open the **File** menu, and click **Open Project**. From the Existing tab in the Open Project dialog box, open **Project 5-1**. Your VB environment should look like Figure 5-3.

Save your form as **FontConvertDB** and your project as **Project 5-2**.

**FIGURE 5-3**
Project 5-1

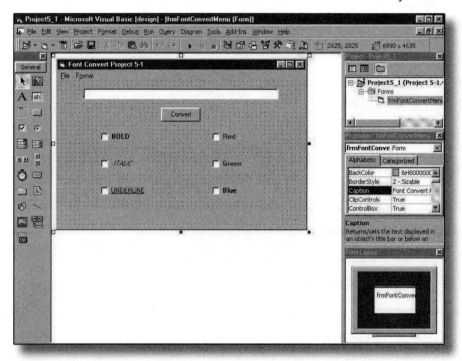

## Step 3: Modify Your Controls

Change the properties of the following controls:

| Control | Property | Value |
|---------|----------|-------|
| Project | Name | Project5_2 |
| Form | Name | frmFontConvertDB |
| | Caption | Font Convert Project 5-2 |

## Step 4: Add the Microsoft Common Dialog Control 6.0/5.0

Open the Project menu in the VB window. Click the **Components** option on the submenu. In the Components dialog box, scroll down the list box items until you find the **Microsoft Common Dialog Control 6.0**, or the **Microsoft Common Dialog Control 5.0** in Visual Basic 5.0. Click in the check box and then click **OK**. The control will be added to the bottom of this project's Toolbox.

## Step 5: Add the Common Dialog Box Control to Your Form

Double-click on the **Common Dialog Box** control in your toolbox. VB will add the control to the middle of your form. You can move this control out of the way of your other controls by clicking and dragging it. However, when the command is selected, the dialog box will open in the middle of your form regardless of where you place it.

### HOT TIP

Because of the common dialog box's chameleon-like ability to take on multiple characteristics, it is possible to use one dialog box control for multiple purposes. The characteristics change through your code.

You cannot resize this control. It will take on the characteristics of the type dialog box you code.

Your dialog box control will not show when your program is run. It will not appear until it is triggered by an event. In this program the event will be clicking the Font option on the Format menu.

Once you have added the dialog box control, your form should look like Figure 5-4.

**FIGURE 5-4**
Project 5-2

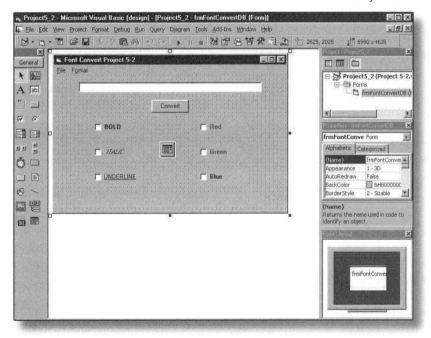

You need to change two properties of the dialog box before you add your code. The properties that need to be changed are as follows:

| Control | Property | Value |
| --- | --- | --- |
| CommonDialog | Name | cdbFont |
| | CancelError | True |

The **cdb** prefix denotes that it is a Common Dialog Box. The "Font" implies that you will be using it as a Font dialog box. Setting the CancelError property to "True" will allow you to control the Cancel button in the dialog box.

**Step 6: Add Code to Your Event**

The event that will trigger the execution of your Font dialog box is a click on the Font option on the Format menu. Therefore, that is where you must enter your code.

Click the **Format** menu option on your form's menu bar, and then click the **Font** option. When the code window opens, add the following code:

```
Private Sub mnuFormatFont_Click()

    On Error GoTo cdbErrHandler
```

The "On Error GoTo" line of code is a VB command. If an error should occur, then the program will go to the **code label** that follows the VB command. A code label occurs inside your code and directs the execution of your program to a specific, or labeled, block of code. In this case, when the user clicks the Cancel button in the Font dialog box, the On Error GoTo command will transfer control to the block of code that follows the cdbErrHandler code label. This block of code will be entered at the end of this procedure.

Now add the following block of code to your procedure:

```
cdbFont.Flags = cdlCFBoth + cdlCFEffects
cdbFont.ShowFont
```

The cdbFont.Flags property is assigned the value of two **flag values**. The **cdlCFBoth** flag will list the available printer and screen fonts in the dialog box. The **cdlCFEffects** flag will let the dialog box enable strikethrough, underline, and color effects. These flags need to be set before we call the **Show method**.

The **ShowFont method** will display the correct type of dialog box, which, in this case, is the Font dialog box.

Now add the following block of code to your procedure:

```
lblChanged.Font.Name = cdbFont.FontName
lblChanged.Font.Size = cdbFont.FontSize
lblChanged.Font.Bold = cdbFont.FontBold
lblChanged.Font.Italic = cdbFont.FontItalic
lblChanged.Font.Underline = cdbFont.FontUnderline
lblChanged.Font.Strikethrough = cdbFont.FontStrikethru
lblChanged.ForeColor = cdbFont.Color
```

Analyze the code you are adding.

**1.** Explain the preceding block of code.

_____

_____

The last part of the code that needs to be added is for error handling. Add the following code label and code to this procedure.

```
cdbErrHandler:
    Exit Sub
End Sub
```

**108**

The cdbErrHandler: is the code label. Notice that it ends with a colon (:). This helps define cdbErrHandler as a code label. The line "Exit Sub" is the command performed when the user clicks the Cancel button in the Font dialog box. The "End Sub" is the ending wrapper line for this procedure.

The code typed within the procedure should look like this:

```
Private Sub mnuFormatFont_Click()

    On Error GoTo cdbErrHandler

    cdbFont.Flags = cdlCFBoth + cdlCFEffects
    cdbFont.ShowFont
    lblChanged.Font.Name = cdbFont.FontName
    lblChanged.Font.Size = cdbFont.FontSize
    lblChanged.Font.Bold = cdbFont.FontBold
    lblChanged.Font.Italic = cdbFont.FontItalic
    lblChanged.Font.Underline = cdbFont.FontUnderline
    lblChanged.Font.Strikethrough = cdbFont.FontStrikethru
    lblChanged.ForeColor = cdbFont.Color

cdbErrHandler:
    Exit Sub
End Sub
```

### Step 5: Save Your Project

Save your project changes by clicking the **Save** button on your toolbar.

### Step 6: Run Your Program

Click the **Run** button on the toolbar to run your program. The program should run exactly as it did in Project 5-1. The only difference is that the Font option on the Format menu will now open a Font dialog box.

### Step 7: Review Your Code

Now that your program has run successfully, answer the following questions. Review your answers with your classmates and teacher.

**1.** Explain how to add the Microsoft Common Dialog Control to your project toolbox.

_____

_____

_____

_____

**2.** Explain how you would use the same dialog box control to execute multiple dialog boxes.

_____

_____

_____

_____

**1 0 9**

**3.** Explain the CancelError property.

_____

_____

_____

**4.** Explain the ShowFont procedure.

_____

_____

**5.** Explain the Flags property.

_____

_____

**6.** Explain how to control the Cancel button in a dialog box.

_____

_____

_____

## P R O J E C T   5 - 3 : Mouse Events   Ⓑ

*Mouse events* are the things you do with the mouse while running an application. Windows sends these events to your program so that you are able to use them. The most obvious and commonly used event is the single click.

In this project you will code multiple mouse events. You will use the Click, Double-Click, Drag-and-Drop, and *MouseDown* (which will allow you to recognize the *right*-click) controls. You will also be introduced to the *PictureBox* control. The events you use in this project can be applied in any application.

### Step 1: Start Your Compiler

Start your compiler if necessary.

### Step 2: Create a New Project

Open the **File** menu, and click **New Project**. When the New Project window appears, double-click the **Standard EXE** button. The Project1 file opens, displaying a blank form named Form1.

### Step 3: Add Your Controls

For this project you will need five PictureBox controls. Resize your form and place your controls as shown in Figure 5-5.

**FIGURE 5-5**
Adding PictureBox controls

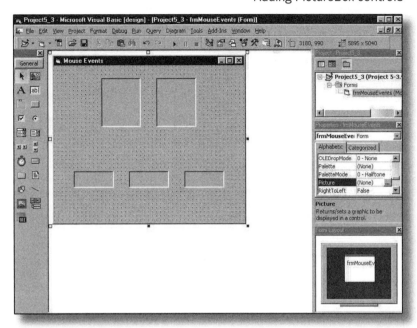

Change the appropriate properties for each control as outlined in the following chart. The picture files are contained in the Student Data & Resources files for this course.

| Control | Property | Value |
|---------|----------|-------|
| Project | Name | Project5_3 |
| Form | Name | frmMouseEvents |
|  | Caption | Mouse Events |
| Picture1 | Name | picOne |
|  | Picture | None |
| Picture2 | Name | picTwo |
|  | Picture | None |
| Picture3 | Name | picThree |
|  | DragMode | Automatic |
|  | Picture | Rolodex.wmf |
| Picture4 | Name | picFour |
|  | DragMode | Automatic |
|  | Picture | Satelit2.wmf |
| Picture5 | Name | picFive |
|  | DragMode | Manual |
|  | Picture | None |

**Step 4: Save Your Project**

Save your project changes by clicking the **Save** button on the toolbar. Your form should look similar to Figure 5-6.

**FIGURE 5-6**

Project 5-3 Mouse Events form

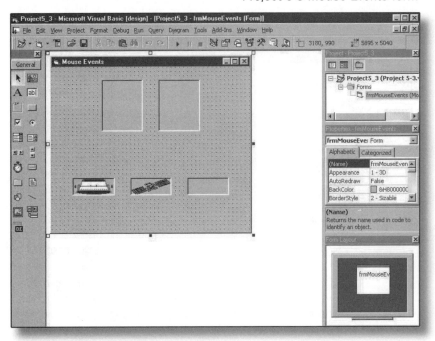

### Step 5: Add Code to Your PictureBox Controls

You now need to add code to your PictureBox controls. The reason you are using PictureBox controls instead of *Image* controls is that the PictureBox is a much more robust control. The pictures used in the PictureBox are automatically resized to fit your box; the Image control actually changes its size to fit the picture size. Both types of controls support the following graphics files:

| | |
|---|---|
| Bitmaps | .bmp |
| Cursors | .cur |
| GIF Files | .gif |
| Icons | .ico |
| JPEG | .jpg or .jpeg |
| Meta-files | .wmf or .emf |
| Run-Length Encoded | .rle |

You will be adding mouse events to your PictureBox controls. Your program will know how to differentiate between the events due to the procedure that you code. And you will find that you can add multiple mouse events to one control. However, adding MouseDown or MouseUp to the same control as the Click and Double-Click events can create problems. Make sure you do not mix those events.

You will need to double-click each PictureBox control in order to enter the necessary code for each event. The Form window editing area will open to display the code attached to each PictureBox. Keep in mind that you will be entering multiple events for some boxes. When you double-click that particular PictureBox, your cursor will be placed in the section of code that you have already entered. All you need to do is select the next procedure that you will be coding from the procedure list box.

**112**

LESSON 5

Figure 5-7 shows the code for the picOne click event. You will be provided screen shots for the remaining code to be added to the PictureBoxes. Make sure you pay attention to the Object and Procedure list boxes so that you enter your code within the proper wrapper lines. Enter your code as it is shown in Figures 5-7, 5-8, 5-9, and 5-10. Make sure you save your project often.

**FIGURE 5-7**
picOne Click event code

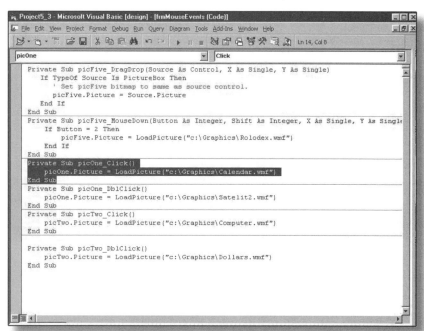

**FIGURE 5-8**
picOne Double-Click event code

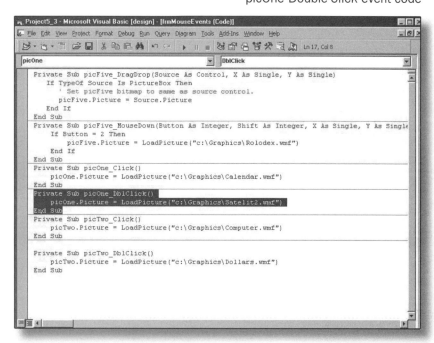

**FIGURE 5-9**

picTwo Click event code

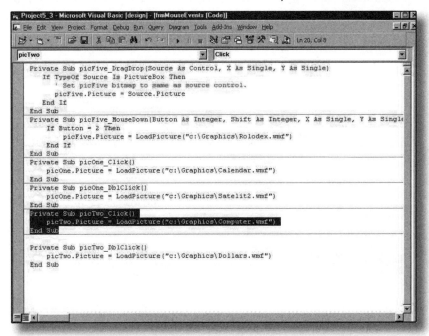

**FIGURE 5-10**

picTwo Double-Click event code

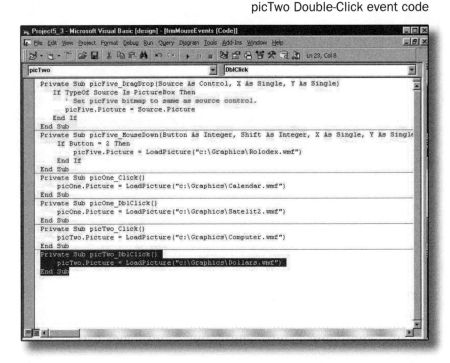

The four blocks of code shown in the figures perform similar tasks. Both the click and double-click events will utilize the **LoadPicture** function to assign a **metafile (.wmf)** to the PictureBox's **Picture** property. The path shown in this example must be replaced with the correct path to the file on your system. Your teacher will tell you where to find these or other graphics files.

Each event will display a different file in the PictureBox depending on the PictureBox and depending on whether the user clicks or double-clicks the mouse. Once you have your code typed in, try your mouse events on these controls.

Now you need to enter the code for the picFive PictureBox drag-and-drop procedure. The code is shown in Figure 5-11.

**FIGURE 5-11**

picFive DragDrop event code

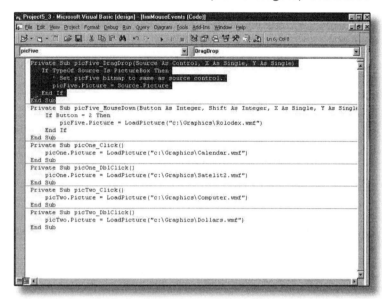

This block of code does not work alone. Even though it is assigned to the picFive PictureBox, the picThree and picFour boxes had to have their **DragMode** property changed. The DragMode for those two PictureBoxes has been set to Automatic. The picFive PictureBox DragMode has been set to Manual. The picThree and picFour PictureBoxes have also had pictures assigned to them in their Properties window.

Both the block of code and the PictureBox properties allow the user to click on the picture shown in either the picThree or picFour box and drag it into the picFive box. The following line of code ensures that we are dealing with a PictureBox control:

```
If TypeOf Source Is PictureBox Then
```

You will now add an additional event to the picFive control. You will be adding a right mouse click event. The code for this event is shown in Figure 5-12.

**FIGURE 5-12**
picFive MouseDown (right-click) event code

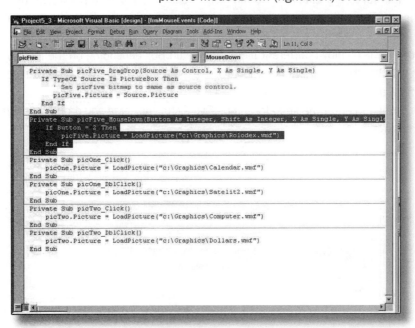

This last block of code is the most difficult, but VB provides you with a great deal of the code. VB supplies you with the following wrapper lines:

```
Private Sub picFive_MouseDown(Button As Integer, Shift As Integer, X As
Single, Y As Single)


End Sub
```

This first line of code is also the same for the MouseUp and the MouseMove events. The Button variable allows you to test for which mouse button had been pressed. A button variable of "1" designates that the left button has been pressed; a value of "2" designates the right button; and a value of "4" designates that both buttons have been pressed. The Shift variable allows you to test for the Shift, Alt, and Ctrl keys being pressed. The *X* and *Y* variables are to hold screen co-ordinates.

The code you added, shown in the following gray box, tests for a right mouse click (If Button = 2). If a right mouse click does occur, the "Rolodex" picture is displayed. The reason you are placing the right click on this control is that it would conflict if placed on controls that already have click and double-click events.

```
If Button = 2 Then
    picFive.Picture = LoadPicture("c:\Graphics\Rolodex.wmf")
End If
```

Again save your project after typing in the code for this mouse event. Now you can run your program.

**116**

### Step 6: Run the Program

Click the **Run** button on the toolbar to run the program. Your program should open in the middle of the screen.

If you click **picOne**, the Calendar picture should appear. Double-clicking **picOne** displays the Satelit2 picture. If you click **picTwo**, the Computer picture displays. Double-clicking **picTwo** displays the Dollar picture.

You can drag either of the pictures in picThree and picFour into picFive. And if you right-click picFive, the Rolodex picture displays. These are all simple events with quite a bit of power. In this project you had fun, but you can apply these mouse events in any program you code.

# Summary

In this lesson you learned how to work with the Menu Editor—a tool separate from the Toolbox but very similar in nature. You created menu options that behaved just like the other controls you have created. You named your options, created accelerator keys for the options, and then added code to the options. Your menu duplicated other controls on your form, but the options allowed you and the user to use the keyboard. This is an important feature of Windows programs—users must be able to use the keyboard if they choose or if the mouse fails.

You then added a Common Dialog Box control to the same program. You learned that this control is actually six dialog boxes in one, depending on the code you use. You added a Font dialog box that again duplicated some of the controls on your form. However, this box placed most of the options in one easy-to-access place.

The last project enabled you to experiment with mouse events—the click, double-click, right-click, and the drag-and-drop operation. You used PictureBox controls and picture files to demonstrate the use of multiple events on single controls. Even though this project was simple and fun, it demonstrated the power of mouse events, which can be used in any application you write.

## LESSON 5 REVIEW QUESTIONS

### SHORT ANSWER

**Define the following in the space provided.**

1. Menus

2. Submenus

**3.** Menu bar

_____

**4.** Accelerator keys

_____

_____

_____

**5.** Checked menu options

_____

_____

**6.** Common dialog box

_____

_____

_____

**7.** Font dialog box

_____

_____

**8.** Mouse events

_____

_____

**9.** Click

_____

**10.** Double-click

_____

**11.** Right-click

_____

_____

**12.** Drag-and-drop

_____

_____

**13.** Menu Editor

_____

**14.** Menu properties

_____

_____

**15.** Menu control list box

_____

_____

**16.** Enabled property

_____

**17.** Visible property

_____

**18.** Ampersand

_____

_____

_____

**19.** mnu

_____

**20.** Ellipsis

_____

_____

**21.** Wrapper lines

_____

_____

**22.** Named constant

_____

_____

**23.** vbRed

_____

**24.** CancelError property

_____

_____

_____

**25.** Code label

_____

_____

**26.** Flag values

_____

**27.** Show method

_____

_____

**28.** ShowFont method

_____

**29.** PictureBox control

_____

_____

**30.** Picture property

_____

_____

**31.** Image control

_____

_____

_____

**32.** LoadPicture function

_____

**33.** DragMode property

_____

_____

## WRITTEN QUESTIONS

**Write your answers to the following questions in the space provided.**

1. Explain why the Menu Editor is not included in the Toolbox.

   _____

   _____

2. Explain the differences between the Toolbox controls and menu options.

   _____

3. Explain checked menu options.

   _____

4. Explain why it is possible to use one Common Dialog Box control to display the six different types of dialog box.

   _____

   _____

   _____

5. Explain why the MouseDown and MouseUp events conflict with the Click and Double-click events.

   _____

6. Explain how to create an accelerator key.

   _____

   _____

7. Explain the use of accelerator keys.

   _____

   _____

   _____

8. Explain wrapper lines.

   _____

   _____

9. Explain named constants and provide two examples.

   _____

   _____

**10.** Explain the use of the CancelError property.

_____

_____

_____

**11.** Explain code labels and provide an example.

_____

_____

_____

**12.** Explain the difference between PictureBox and Image controls.

_____

_____

**13.** Explain why the DragMode property of picThree and picFour needed to be set to Automatic.

_____

_____

**14.** Explain the LoadPicture function.

_____

# TESTING YOUR SKILLS

 **Estimated Time:**

Application 5-1  1 $^{1}/_{2}$ hours
Application 5-2  45 minutes

## APPLICATION 5-1

In Project 5-2 you added a Font dialog box to your font conversion program. In this application you will add another common dialog box—the Color dialog box.

**1.** Open your **Project 5-2**. Save the form as **FontConvertApp**, and save your project as **App5-1**.

**2.** Rename your project and form within the project to match the filenames.

**3.** Remove the three options from the Color submenu option.

**4.** Add a second Common Dialog Box control to your form to be used as the Color dialog box. Name it accordingly.

**5.** Add the code to show the Color dialog box to the Color submenu option, which is on the Format menu. Also add the code to change the font color of the text to be displayed.

**6.** Save your project.

**7.** Run your project to test it. Then debug it if necessary. Run it again.

**122**

## APPLICATION 5-2

In this application you will add another mouse event to the picOne control in Project 5-3.

1. Open your **Project 5-3**. Save the form as **MouseEventsApp**, and save your project as **App5-2**.

2. Rename your project and form within the project to match the new filenames.

3. Add the code to the picOne control to respond to a right mouse click. A right mouse click should display the Rolodex picture.

4. If you need help with the code, review the MouseDown event for picFive.

5. Save your project.

6. Run your project to test it. Then debug it if necessary. Run it again.

7. Observe what happens when you right-click picOne. Compare it to what happens when you right-click picFive. Explain the difference.

_____

_____

_____

_____

_____

## CRITICAL THINKING

**Estimated Time: 6 hours**

Combine **Project 3-4**: simple interest, **Application 3-1**: discounted interest, and **Project 4-6**: compound interest into one multiple-form application. The main form will provide a choice between simple interest and compound interest. Compound interest will have its own form. The simple interest and the discounted interest will occupy the same form. They will share the same labels, text boxes, and command buttons. The user will choose between the calculations through menu choices. The code behind the menu choices will also modify the controls so that they represent the calculation chosen by the user. The only form that is allowed to exit the program is the main form.

# BASIC DATA MANIPULATION

LESSON

6

## OBJECTIVES

**Upon completion of this lesson, you should be able to:**

- Explain arrays.

- Declare and initialize arrays.

- Display array output.

- Access arrays using subscripts.

- Perform a bubble sort.

- Perform a data search.

🕐 **Estimated Time: 8 hours**

## *Introduction*

This lesson provides you with the tools to perform *data manipulation* within *memory*. Many applications are created to manipulate data. The data are usually stored on a *mass storage device*, such as a *hard drive*, *CD-ROM*, or a *DVD*. The *access times* of these devices are notoriously slow when compared to manipulating data stored in *physical memory*. By initially placing your data into memory or loading it from your storage device into memory, you can drastically decrease your "handling time." *Arrays* are tools that do just that—they provide temporary storage areas in memory that typically hold data of the same name and type.

Arrays are *declared* and *initialized* like any other variable; however, more memory areas are associated with an array. Arrays can be declared with the *Public statement* if you want them to be used throughout your application. If you want to use them within a module, you will declare the array with the *Dim statement*. Arrays also need to be named. If you wish, you can add an *ar* prefix to differentiate your arrays.

Arrays can hold a great many variables. But how do they differentiate between the items, or *elements*, if they are all the same name and type? You will learn to use *subscripts* to access the elements in an array. A subscript is simply the numeric value of the position in the array where the element "lives." Arrays begin their subscript numbering with *zero*. However, Visual Basic programmers like to begin their arrays with *one*. You will learn how to modify VB to let you do this.

From there you will use *parallel arrays*, perform a *bubble sort*, and search for array elements. This is one of the advantages to using arrays. By manipulating your data in memory, you can speed up the performance of your applications.

**125**

This lesson will focus on the following:

- **Explaining, declaring, and initializing arrays.** You will be creating and using arrays in the projects in this lesson.

- **Displaying array output.** You will display the output of your manipulations. Because it is nearly impossible to watch the data being manipulated in memory, it makes sense to allow your users to see the results of the procedures and applications.

- **Accessing arrays using subscripts.** In order to place data into your array and to later manipulate it, you must be able to find the data. You will utilize subscripts to retrieve data from your array elements.

- **Performing a bubble sort.** At times users must put their information into some sort of order. The data are usually sorted in a low-to-high order known as *ascending,* or in a high-to-low order known as *descending*. This order can be applied to all kinds of data because all data are truly numeric in nature.

- **Performing a data search.** To retrieve specific pieces of data, users first must be able to find the data. You will create a project that performs a data search.

## P R O J E C T  6 - 1 : Simple Array

In this project you create a simple array that allows the user to input five elements and then display them. You will learn how to use the **InputBox()** function, which allows you to prompt the user for input with one message box. The InputBox() function returns a Variant data type from the text box provided for user input. The data can easily be interpreted as a **string**. With one line of code, you can place a title on the box, provide a user prompt, provide a text box for data entry, and provide OK and Cancel buttons.

As the user inputs the requested data through the input box, your program will enter the data into an array. Each element will be placed into the array in the order it is input. You will use a For loop and a subscript to input the data into each element.

You will display the results of the data input to your array with the **MessageBox()** function, which produces a pop-up message box. The message box you will use displays a message for the user and provides at least one command button. In this project the message box will display the data input by the user and provide an OK button with which the user can continue.

You will also notice one other difference with the code in this project. The code is not attached to a control on a form. The code is contained in a separate **code module**. Because this procedure is not linked to a specific control, it is known as a **general procedure**. You can call this procedure from anywhere in your application because it will be declared as a Public procedure.

### Step 1: Start Your Compiler

Start your compiler if it is not already running.

## Step 2: Create a New Project

Open the **File** menu and click **New Project**. In the New Project window, double-click the **Standard EXE** button. The Project1 file opens, displaying a blank form named Form1.

## Step 3: Add Your Code

For this project you will not need any controls, only code. You can leave your form the size it is. The first thing you will need to do is change the following properties for your project and your form.

| Control | Property | Value |
|---------|----------|-------|
| Project | Name | Project6_1 |
| Form | Name | frmCodeHolder |
| | Caption | Code Holder |

Even though the user will not see this form, it is good to program consistently.

You now need to add your code. Because the code you will be entering does not belong to a specific control, you will need to open a code module. Click the **Project** option on your VB menu bar and then click the **Add Module** option on the submenu. The correct selection is highlighted in Figure 6-1.

**FIGURE 6-1**
Add Module submenu option

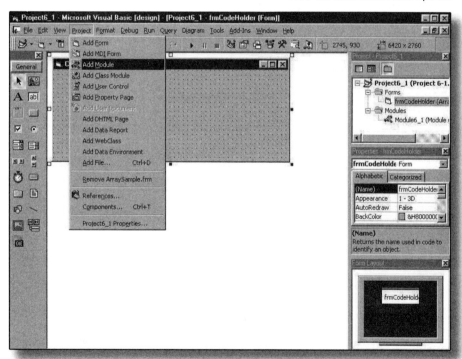

The Add Module dialog box opens, as shown in Figure 6-2.

**FIGURE 6-2**
Add Module dialog box

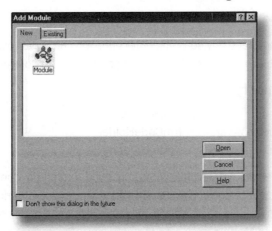

The New tab is selected by default. Click the **Open** button. A code editing window opens, and the (General) object and the (Declarations) procedure are shown in the drop-down list boxes at the top of the window. See Figure 6-3.

**FIGURE 6-3**
Add Module code editing window

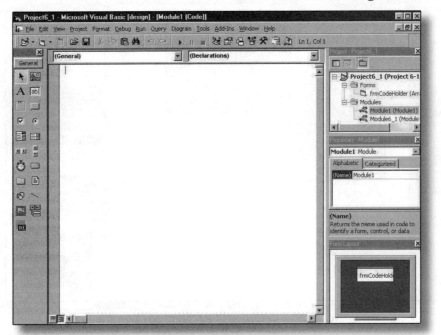

**128**

You will enter your code in this window. Figure 6-4 shows the code that needs to be entered.

**FIGURE 6-4**
Array code—BestFriends general procedure

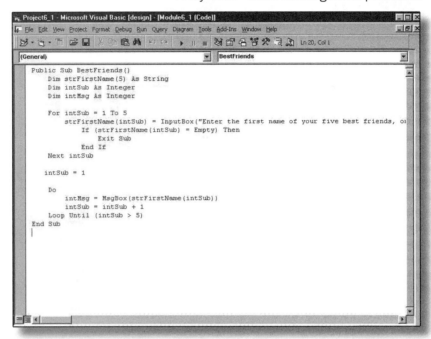

The first line of code within the For loop is rather long, so it is shown in the following box for readability:

```
For intSub = 1 To 5
      strFirstName(intSub) = InputBox("Enter the first name
             of your five best friends, one at a time.",
             "Best Friends")
          If (strFirstName(intSub) = Empty) Then
             Exit Sub
          End If
  Next intSub
```

This block of code executes the entire program with the exception of calling the procedure. The next code that needs to be added is the ***procedure call***.

Double-click the form icon in the Project window. Your 'frmCodeHolder' will open in the Form window editing area. Double-click on your form so that the code-editing window opens. The Form object and Load procedure are listed in the drop-down list boxes at the top of the window. Type in the code as shown in Figure 6-5.

**FIGURE 6-5**
Procedure call

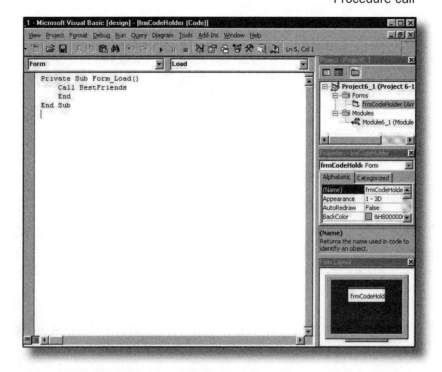

```
Private Sub Form_Load()
        Call BestFriends
        End
End Sub
```

Your code is now complete.

### Step 4: Save Your Project

Change the Module1 Name property to **Module6_1**. Then save your project using **Save As**. When prompted, save your form as **CodeHolder**, your module as **Module 6-1**, and your project as **Project 6-1**.

### Step 5: Run the Program

Click the **Run** button on the toolbar to run your program, which should open in the middle of the screen. You will notice that your form never shows. You will be prompted to Enter the first name of your five best friends, one at a time, with an input box. The OK button will cause the loop to proceed. Once you have entered the names of your five best friends, you will have the results displayed with five separate message boxes. If you select the Cancel button, the program will end.

### Step 6: Review Your Code

Now that your program has run successfully, answer the following questions. Review your answers with your classmates and teacher.

**1.** Explain the purpose of the InputBox().

_____

_____

_____

_____

**2.** Explain the purpose of the MessageBox().

_____

_____

**3.** Explain the difference between a Private and a Public procedure.

_____

_____

**4.** Explain the use of general procedures.

_____

_____

**5.** Explain why the CodeHolder form is never displayed.

_____

_____

_____

**6.** Explain the following block of code:

```
Public Sub BestFriends()
    Dim strFirstName(5) As String
    Dim intSub As Integer
    Dim intMsg As Integer
```

_____

_____

_____

_____

**7.** Explain the following For loop:

```
For intSub = 1 To 5
    strFirstName(intSub) = InputBox("Enter the first name
            of your five best friends, one at a time.",
            "Best Friends")
        If (strFirstName(intSub) = Empty) Then
            Exit Sub
        End If
Next intSub
```

_____

_____

_____

**131**

**8.** Explain the following block of code:

```
    intSub = 1

    Do
    intMsg = MsgBox(strFirstName(intSub))
    intSub = intSub + 1
    Loop Until (intSub > 5)
End Sub
```

_____

_____

_____

_____

_____

**9.** Explain the following procedure call:

```
Private Sub Form_Load()
    Call BestFriends
    End
End Sub
```

_____

_____

You have coded your first array.

## P R O J E C T   6 - 2 : Parallel Arrays

In this project you will add another code module to Project 6-1. This code module will execute parallel arrays. Each array will hold its own data type; however, the data in the corresponding element position of the two arrays will be related to each other.

You will also modify your CodeHolder form to act as a selection menu. All of your general procedures will be called from your menu form.

### Step 1: Start Your Compiler

Start your compiler if necessary.

## Step 2: Open Project 6-1

Open the **File** menu and click **Open Project**. In the Open Project dialog box, open your **Project 6-1** Project from the Existing tab. Your VB environment should look like Figure 6-6.

**FIGURE 6-6**
Project 6-1

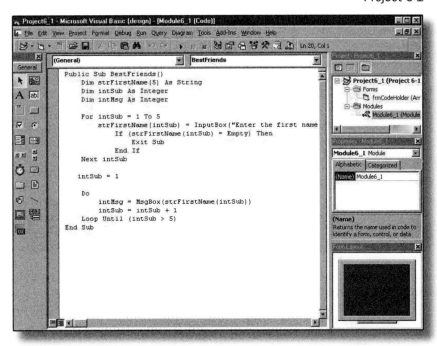

Immediately save your form as **ProcedureMenu**, your module as **ModuleSimpleArray**, and your project as **Project 6-2**.

Rename your existing controls as follows:

| Control | Property | Value |
|---|---|---|
| Project | Name | Project6_2 |
| Form | Name | frmProcedureMenu |
| | Caption | Procedure Menu Project 6-2 |
| Module | Name | Module6_2 |

Save your project once again by clicking the **Save** button on the toolbar.

## Step 3: Modify Your Form

Double-click your form icon in the Project window to open the form in the Form window editing area. Resize your form and add five command buttons, as shown in Figure 6-7.

**FIGURE 6-7**
Procedure Menu form

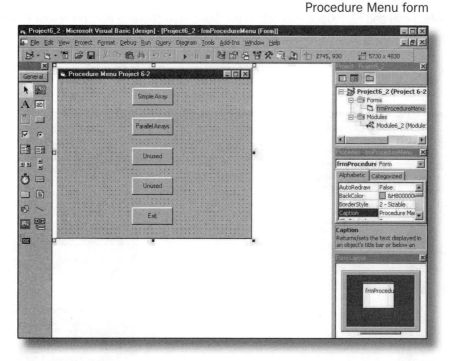

**1.** Write the names you give to your command buttons in the following spaces:

| Control | Property | Value |
|---|---|---|
| Command1 | Name | _____ |
| | Caption | Simple Array |
| Command2 | Name | _____ |
| | Caption | Parallel Arrays |
| Command3 | Name | _____ |
| | Caption | Unused |
| Command4 | Name | _____ |
| | Caption | Unused |
| Command5 | Name | _____ |
| | Caption | Exit |

The first command button will call the BestFriends general procedure, which is Module 6-2. The second command button will call the new parallel arrays general procedure you will be coding. The third and fourth buttons will be unused until later. The fifth command button will allow you to Exit the program.

**Step 4: Cut and Paste Your BestFriends General Procedure**

Cut and paste the procedure call from the Form_Load() event to the **cmdSimpleArray_Click()** event in your code editing window. Delete the **End** statement from the code that you cut and paste.

**Step 5: Add Code to Your Exit Button**

Add the code to your Exit button that will cause the program to terminate when clicked.

**134**

## Step 6: Code Your Parallel Arrays

The only difference between a single, simple array and parallel arrays is that your users will enter different types of data that are related to each other and will be stored in the same element number but in different arrays.

In this project you will enter survey results and the person's name who responded to the survey. First you will need to add a new module to your project. Click the **Project** option on your menu bar. Click the **Add Module** submenu option. In the Add Module dialog box, click the **Open** button on the New tab. The code editing window will open with the (General) object and (Declarations) procedure displayed in the drop-down list boxes at the top of the form. See Figure 6-3.

Rename your new module **Module6_2B**. Copy and paste the code from your BestFriends procedure into your new module. Now modify the existing block of code as shown in Figure 6-8.

**FIGURE 6-8**

Parallel Array—SurveyResults general procedure

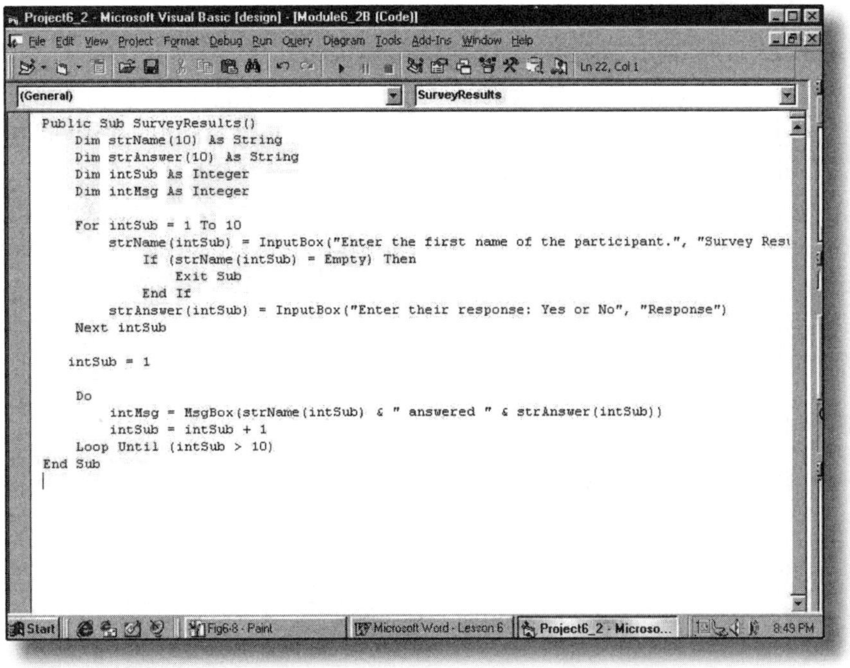

The first line of code within the For loop is rather long, so it is shown in the following box for readability:

```
For intSub = 1 To 10
        strName(intSub) = InputBox("Enter the first name of
                the participant.", "Survey Results")
            If (strName(intSub) = Empty) Then
                Exit Sub
            End If
        strAnswer(intSub) = InputBox("Enter their response:
                Yes or No", "Response")
    Next intSub
```

This block of code executes the entire program with the exception of calling the procedure. Now you need to add the procedure call to the cmdParallelArray command button.

1. Write the code you will add to the cmdParallelArray command button to call your new procedure in the following space:

_____

_____

_____

### Step 7: Save Your Project

Save your project changes by clicking the **Save** button on the toolbar. In the Save As dialog box, save your new module as **Module 6-2B**. Once you save your new module, the rest of the project components and the project itself will be saved automatically.

### Step 8: Run Your Program

Click the **Run** button on the toolbar to run your program. Your program will start with the ProcedureMenu form. When you click the Simple Array command button, the BestFriends general procedure will execute just as it did in Project 6-1. When you click the Parallel Arrays command button, the SurveyResults general procedure will execute.

The SurveyResults parallel array will prompt you for the name of the survey participant and his or her response, which should be Yes or No. Once you enter 10 names and 10 results, the data are displayed to you, combined in one message box. The OK and Cancel buttons will be functional as they were for the BestFriends simple array.

You now have a program that demonstrates two different types of arrays.

### Step 9: Review Your Code

Now that your program has run successfully, answer the following questions. Review your answers with your classmates and teacher.

1. Explain the major differences between the simple array code and the parallel array code.

_____

_____

_____

2. Write the code that causes the Cancel button to execute properly on the InputBox. Explain how this code performs.

_____

_____

_____

3. Explain why you need only one subscript for both arrays.

_____

_____

**4.** Explain why you needed to change the name of the strFirstName variable to strName for the SurveyResults general procedure.

_____

_____

## P R O J E C T  6 - 3 : Bubble Sort

Bubble sorts put your data in a specific order, which either increases in value (ascending) or decreases in value (descending). Either way, users should make the choice because they are the ones who use the data. For example, sorting data is very useful in presorting bulk mailings. By presorting bulk mailings, businesses achieve lower postal rates.

Bubble sorts are so called because the smaller values will eventually "bubble" to the top of the list (ascending order). In this project you will create a bubble sort. You will use a For loop within a For loop to make sure the proper values bubble to the top. The outer/inner For loop combination ensures that each value in the array is processed and placed in its proper order. A single For loop would result in only one value being placed in the proper position.

### Step 1: Start Your Compiler

Start your compiler if necessary.

### Step 2: Open Project 6-2

Open the **File** menu, and click **Open Project**. In the Open Project dialog box, open **Project 6-2** from the Existing tab. Your VB environment should look like Figure 6-9.

**FIGURE 6-9**
Project 6-2

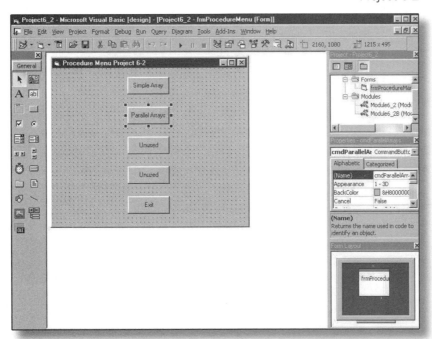

Immediately save your form as **ProcedureMenu2**, your modules as **ModuleSimpleArray2** and **ModuleParallelArray** (was Module 6-2B), and your project as **Project 6-3**.

Rename your existing controls as follows:

| Control | Property | Value |
| --- | --- | --- |
| Project | Name | Project6_3 |
| Form | Name | frmProcedureMenu2 |
| | Caption | Procedure Menu Project 6-3 |
| Module6_2 | Name | Module6_3 |
| Module6_2B | Name | Module6_3B |

Save your project once again by clicking the **Save** button on the toolbar.

### Step 3: Code Your Bubble Sort

In this project you will perform a bubble sort on an array. First you need to add a new module to your project. Click the **Project** option on your menu bar. Click the **Add Module** submenu option. In the Add Module dialog box, make sure the **New** tab is selected, and click the **Open** button. The code editing window will open, with the (General) object and (Declarations) procedure displayed in the drop-down list boxes at the top of the form. See Figure 6-3.

Rename your new module **Module6_3C**. Add the block of code shown in the following box.

```
Public Sub BubbleSort()
    Dim strFirstName(5) As String
    Dim strSwap As String
    Dim intSub As Integer
    Dim intInnerSub As Integer
    Dim intSubNext As Integer
    Dim intMsg As Integer

    For intSub = 1 To 5
        strFirstName(intSub) = InputBox("Enter the first name
            of your five best friends, one at a time.",
            "Best Friends")
            If (strFirstName(intSub) = Empty) Then
                Exit Sub
            End If
    Next intSub

    intSub = 1
    intInnerSub = 1
    intSubNext = 1

    For intSub = 1 To 4
        For intInnerSub = 1 To 4
            intSubNext = intInnerSub + 1
            If (strFirstName(intInnerSub) >
                        strFirstName(intSubNext)) Then
                strSwap = strFirstName(intInnerSub)
                strFirstName(intInnerSub) =
                        strFirstName(intSubNext)
                strFirstName(intSubNext) = strSwap
```

```
            End If
        Next intInnerSub
    Next intSub

    intSub = 1

    Do
        intMsg = MsgBox(strFirstName(intSub))
        intSub = intSub + 1
    Loop Until (intSub > 5)
End Sub
```

Before this procedure will actually run, you need to call it from the proper command button. Rename your cmdUnused1command button to **cmdBubbleSort**, and then change the Caption property to **Bubble Sort**. Then add the code needed to call the procedure to the command button. Write the code you attach to the command button in the following space:

_____

_____

_____

### Step 4: Save Your Project

Save your project changes by clicking the **Save** button on the toolbar. In the Save As dialog box, save your new module as **ModuleBubbleSort**. Once you save your new module, the rest of the project components and the project itself are saved automatically.

### Step 5: Run the Program

Click the **Run** button on the toolbar to run the program. Your menu form will execute. Test both the Simple Array and the Parallel Arrays buttons to make sure they work as they have. Then click the **Bubble Sort** button.

You will be prompted to enter the names of your five best friends. When your best friends' names are displayed back to you, they will be in ascending alphabetical order.

### Step 6: Review Your Code

Now that your program has run successfully, answer the following questions. Review your answers with your classmates and teacher.

**1**. Explain the purpose of these four variables:

```
Dim strSwap As String
Dim intSub As Integer
Dim intInnerSub As Integer
Dim intSubNext As Integer
```

_____

_____

_____

**139**

**2.** Explain these three assignment statements:

```
intSub = 1
intInnerSub = 1
intSubNext = 1
```

_____

**3.** Explain the bubble sort code block.

```
For intSub = 1 To 4
    For intInnerSub = 1 To 4
        intSubNext = intInnerSub + 1
        If (strFirstName(intInnerSub) >
                    strFirstName(intSubNext)) Then
            strSwap = strFirstName(intInnerSub)
            strFirstName(intInnerSub) =
                    strFirstName(intSubNext)
            strFirstName(intSubNext) = strSwap
        End If
    Next intInnerSub
Next intSub
```

_____

_____

_____

_____

_____

_____

**4.** Explain why the bubble sort For loop counters only go to 4 instead of 5.

_____

_____

_____

You now have an example of how to sort data contained in your arrays.

## PROJECT 6-4 : Searching

Now that you know how to get data into simple and parallel arrays and how to sort the data, you need to be able to find values in your arrays. To do so, you must perform a **_search_** procedure. There are many ways to search—some easy and some difficult. In light of the heavy emphasis in the information technology industry on databases, more efficient search methods are being sought. In fact, some of the leading research in the industry today is being done in the development of search techniques.

Think of the times you have browsed the Internet searching for information. That procedure is no different from what you will program in this project, with the exception of the massive data files being searched. We will use a simple but effective search method in this project. Should this spark a personal interest for you, you may have just found the perfect career!

### Step 1: Start Your Compiler

Start your compiler if necessary.

### Step 2: Open Project 6-3

Open the **File** menu, and click **Open Project**. In the Open Project dialog box, open your **Project 6-3** Project from the Existing tab. Your VB environment should look like Figure 6-10.

**FIGURE 6-10**
Project 6-3

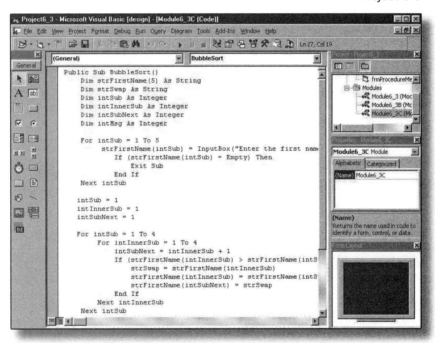

Immediately save your form as **ProcedureMenu3**, your modules as **ModuleSimpleArray3** and **ModuleParallelArray2**, **ModuleBubbleSort2**, and your project as **Project 6-4**.

Rename your existing controls as follows:

| Control | Property | Value |
| --- | --- | --- |
| Project | Name | Project6_4 |
| Form | Name | frmProcedureMenu3 |
| | Caption | Procedure Menu Project 6-4 |
| Module6_3 | Name | Module6_4 |
| Module6_3B | Name | Module6_4B |
| Module6_3C | Name | Module6_4C |

Save your project once again by clicking the **Save** button on the toolbar.

## Step 3: Code Your Bubble Sort

In this project you will perform a search on an array. First add a new module to your project. Rename your new module **Module6_4D**. Then add the block of code as follows:

```
Public Sub Search()
    Dim strFirstName(5) As String
    Dim strSearcher As String
    Dim intSub As Integer
    Dim intFound As Integer
    Dim intMsg As Integer

    intFound = -1

    For intSub = 1 To 5
        strFirstName(intSub) = InputBox("Enter the first name
            of your five best friends, one at a time.",
            "Best Friends")
            If (strFirstName(intSub) = Empty) Then
                Exit Sub
            End If
    Next intSub

    intSub = 1

    strSearcher = InputBox("Enter the name for which you are
            searching: ", "Searcher")

    For intSub = 1 To 5
        If (strFirstName(intSub) = strSearcher) Then
                intFound = intSub
                Exit For
        End If
    Next intSub

    If (intFound <> -1) Then
        intMsg = MsgBox("Your search item " &
            strFirstName(intSub) & " was found in element "
            & intSub & ".")
    Else
        intMsg = MsgBox("Your search item was not found.")
    End If
End Sub
```

Before this procedure will actually run, you will need to call it from the proper command button. Rename your cmdUnused2 command button to **cmdSearch**, and then change the Caption property to **Search**. Then add the code needed to call the procedure to the command button.

**1.** Write the code you attach to the command button in the follwoing space:

_____

_____

_____

**142**

## Step 4: Save Your Project

Save your project changes by clicking the **Save** button on the toolbar. In the Save As dialog box, save your new module as **ModuleSearch**. Once you save your new module, the rest of the project components and the project itself are saved automatically.

## Step 5: Run the Program

Click the **Run** button on the toolbar to run the program. Your menu form will execute. Test the Simple Array, the Parallel Arrays, and the Bubble Sort buttons to make sure they work as they did previously. Then click the **Search** button.

You will be prompted to enter the names of your five best friends. Then you will be prompted for a "searcher"—a name for which you are looking. Once you enter the name for which you are searching and click OK, your program will search for that name. If a match is found, you will be informed as to what array element contains the name. If it is not found, you will be informed that the name for which you are searching cannot be found.

## Step 6: Review Your Code

Now that your program has run successfully, answer the following questions. Review your answers with your classmates and teacher.

**1.** Explain the purpose of these five variables:

```
Dim strFirstName(5) As String
Dim strSearcher As String
Dim intSub As Integer
Dim intFound As Integer
Dim intMsg As Integer
```

_____

_____

_____

_____

_____

_____

**2.** Explain this assignment statement:

```
intFound = -1
```

_____

_____

**3.** Explain the following lines of code:

```
intSub = 1

strSearcher = InputBox("Enter the name for which you are
          searching: ", "Searcher")
```

_____

_____

_____

_____

**4.** Explain the search sequence and the result:

```
For intSub = 1 To 5
    If (strFirstName(intSub) = strSearcher) Then
            intFound = intSub
            Exit For
    End If
Next intSub

If (intFound <> -1) Then
    intMsg = MsgBox("Your search item " &
            strFirstName(intSub) & " was found in element
            " & intSub & ".")
Else
    intMsg = MsgBox("Your search item was not found.")
End If
```

_____

_____

_____

_____

_____

You can now search for data in your arrays.

# *Summary*

In this lesson you practiced basic data manipulation. In a twist from previous projects, you entered all code into modules and then called the modules from a single form. You began your projects in this lesson with an understanding of why it is easier and much more efficient to manipulate data in memory instead of doing it from a storage device. You then created a simple array that requested input from a user and displayed the output. Your simple array used InputBox() and MessageBox() functions to communicate with the user.

You also created a project that accepted related but different data and stored them in parallel arrays. These parallel arrays held matching data in corresponding elements. By doing this you can store different data types in different arrays, yet match the data when needed.

After you created arrays to hold your data, you began the manipulation. You coded two projects that dealt with sorting and searching. Both topics are very important in light of the emphasis on data storage and retrieval in the information technology industry. The sort you performed was a simple but effective bubble sort. The search was a simple "check until you find a match" search.

The projects you created were simple, but they introduced very important topics for use throughout your programming career. Consider them as a stepping stone to more intricate and complex methods.

## LESSON 6 REVIEW QUESTIONS

### SHORT ANSWER

**Define the following in the space provided.**

1. Data manipulation

2. Memory

3. Mass storage devices

4. Hard drive

5. CD-ROM

6. DVD

7. Access times

8. Arrays

**9.** Declared

_____

_____

**10.** Initialized

_____

_____

**11.** Public statement

_____

**12.** Dim statement

_____

**13.** ar

_____

_____

**14.** Subscripts

_____

**15.** Element

_____

**16.** Parallel arrays

_____

_____

**17.** Bubble sort

_____

_____

**18.** InputBox()

_____

_____

_____

**19.** String

_____

**20.** MessageBox()

_____

_____

_____

**21.** Code module

_____

**22.** General procedure

_____

**23.** Public procedure

_____

**24.** Procedure call

_____

**25.** Ascending

_____

**26.** Descending

_____

**27.** Search

_____

## WRITTEN QUESTIONS

**Write your answers to the following questions in the space provided.**

**1.** Explain the difference between a simple array and a parallel array.

_____

_____

_____

**2.** Explain why it is more efficient to manipulate data in memory.

_____

**3.** Explain how to declare an array.

_____

_____

**4.** Explain subscripts and their use.

_____

**5.** Explain code modules.

_____

_____

_____

**6.** Explain the difference in the use of the Public and Dim statements in regard to arrays.

_____

_____

_____

**7.** Explain bubble sort.

_____

_____

**8.** Explain why the upper limits in the For loops in a bubble sort are one less than the array size.

_____

_____

_____

**9.** Write the line of code needed to call a procedure named YourFriends.

_____

**10.** Explain why sorting and searching are hot topics in the computer industry.

_____

_____

_____

_____

# TESTING YOUR SKILLS

 **Estimated Time:**

Application 6-1  1 $\frac{1}{2}$ hours
Application 6-2  1 $\frac{1}{2}$ hours

## APPLICATION 6-1

SCANS

In Project 6-3 you coded a bubble sort module that is also part of Project 6-4. Your module sorted your array data in ascending order. Add a module to your final project, Project 6-4, that will perform a bubble sort in descending order.

**1.** Open **Project 6-4**. Save all of your components with the suffix **App6-1** attached to them, and then save your project as **App6-1**.

**2.** Rename your project and components within the project to match the preceding names.

**148**

3. Add an additional command button for the descending sort. Recaption and rename the Bubble Sort button to Ascending Sort.

4. Add a new code module. Add the code needed for the descending bubble sort.

5. Add the procedure call to your descending sort button.

6. Save your project.

7. Run your project to test it. Then debug it if necessary. Run it again.

## APPLICATION 6-2

In Project 6-2 you coded a parallel array that is also part of Application 6-1. Your module gathered two different types of data into two different arrays. Add a module to your final project, App6-1, that will use a triple parallel array. The third array will be an integer array that will gather the participants' ages.

1. Open your **App6-1**. Save all of your components with the suffix **App6-2** attached to them, then save your project as **App6-2**.

2. Rename your project and components within the project to match the names in item #1.

3. Add an additional command button for the triple array.

4. Add a new code module. Add the code needed for the triple array.

5. Add the procedure call to your triple array.

6. Save your project.

7. Run your project to test it. Then debug it if necessary. Run it again.

## CRITICAL THINKING

Estimated Time: 4 hours

1. Create a parallel array project that will gather input from the user. Collect information from 10 users.

2. Prompt the user for First Name, Last Name, Street Address, City, State, and ZIP.

3. Input the information into six parallel arrays.

4. Display the information entered in mailing label format on the face of a form. Remember the form printing you did in Project 4-5.

# VB AND DATABASES

LESSON 7

## Introduction

Everything you have done so far in this book (and probably in your VB class), has dealt with input, output, and manipulating data in memory. However, even though most program activity takes place in memory, users still need to store data for later use. This lesson addresses that topic.

Files are accessed in either a *sequential* or a *random* manner. In most cases today, *random access* is the norm. However, there are some instances where sequential access is still important. Sequential access is a method of storing data in the order in which it is input. Any data added to a sequential file is then added at the end of the file, or *appended*. Random access is a method of storing data in any order. Data is input and stored wherever, but it is still in the file. And the data are accessible directly, without searching all the other records in the file.

File access is not hard. The methods are simple and straightforward. You begin by designing your project, which has users input information they would like to store. Once a user inputs the information, your program should process it. You have the option of collecting the information in an array and then "writing" the information in the array to a file, or you can write to a file as the user inputs the data. You will code both methods in this lesson.

You will also create an interface for a *Microsoft Access database*. You will use the Visual Basic data control to create an interface to a sample database. This is the only Data control built into VB. There are additional VB data tools available; however, they are specific to the version of VB you are using.

**151**

This lesson focuses on the following:

■ **Entering data into and reading data from a sequential access file.** You will use one of your earlier programs to prompt the user for input and then save the data to a file. You will also display the data input by reading the file you created.

■ **Entering data into and reading data from a random access file.** You will use a form from an earlier project to collect input from users and store it in a random access file. You will display the contents of this file independent of the entry.

■ **Read data from a Microsoft Access database.** You will design a form that will use the Data control to read data from a sample Microsoft Access database. More intricate access is available depending on the version of Visual Basic you use. The Data control will introduce you to concepts you can later expand upon.

 **P R O J E C T   7 - 1 :** Sequential File Write and Read

In this project you will modify Project 6-1 which prompted the user to input the names of his or her five best friends using an input box. The names were input into an array and then displayed immediately after the input by a message box.

In this project you will modify that project slightly. You will still use your only form to call the general procedure that executes the body of the program. But this time your program will use both the *Print #* statement and the *Write #* statement to place the data entered in the array into two different sequential files. Once the data are entered into the files, one of the files will be reopened to display the contents.

You will be able to read the contents of each file independently by using Notepad or another simple word processing program. This is a good way to review the workings of your program. You will learn the steps to do this later in the project.

> **HOT TIP**
>
> Check the file path in your code. Check with your teacher to determine whether this is where your files should be created.

### Step 1: Start Your Compiler

Start your compiler if it is not already running.

### Step 2: Open Project 6-1

Open the **File** menu and click **Open Project**. In the Open Project dialog box, open your **Project 6-1** Project from the Existing tab. Your VB environment should look like Figure 7-1.

**FIGURE 7-1**
Project 6-1

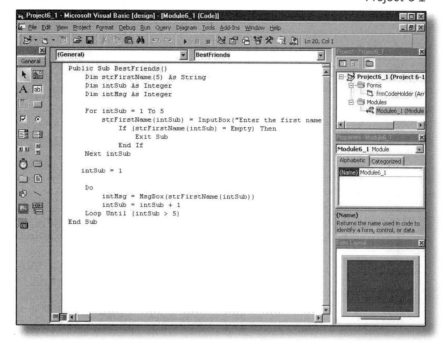

```
Public Sub BestFriends()
    Dim strFirstName(5) As String
    Dim intSub As Integer
    Dim intMsg As Integer

    For intSub = 1 To 5
        strFirstName(intSub) = InputBox("Enter the first name
            If (strFirstName(intSub) = Empty) Then
                Exit Sub
            End If
    Next intSub

    intSub = 1

    Do
        intMsg = MsgBox(strFirstName(intSub))
        intSub = intSub + 1
    Loop Until (intSub > 5)
End Sub
```

Immediately save your form as **SequentialFile**, your module as **ModeSeq7-1**, and your project as **Project 7-1**.

Rename your existing controls as follows:

| Control | Property | Value |
|---------|----------|-------|
| Project | Name | Project7_1 |
| Form | Name | frmSequentialFile |
| | Caption | Sequential File |
| Module | Name | Module7_1 |

Save your project once again by clicking the **Save** button on the toolbar.

### Step 3: Add Your Code

For this project you will not need any additional controls. You will only need to modify your code. You can leave your form the size it is.

Double-click the **Module7_1** icon in the Project window. The code editing window opens to show your existing code. Rename the procedure to **BestFriendsSequential**. Click elsewhere in the window to see the name change take effect in the Procedure list box, as shown in Figure 7-2.

**FIGURE 7-2**
BestFriendsSequential procedure

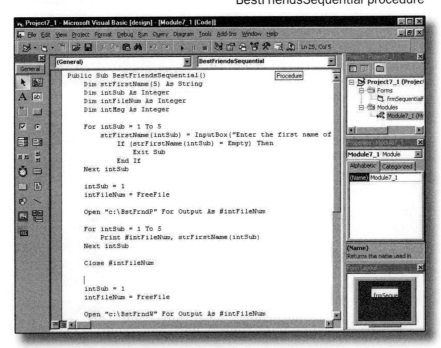

You will now need to modify the code to add the routines necessary to write to both files and to read from one of them. The code is too long to show in a figure, so it is shown in the following box:

```
Public Sub BestFriendsSequential()
    Dim strFirstName(5) As String
    Dim intSub As Integer
    Dim intFileNum As Integer
    Dim intMsg As Integer

    For intSub = 1 To 5
        strFirstName(intSub) = InputBox("Enter the first name
                of your five best friends, one at a time.",
                "Best Friends")
        If (strFirstName(intSub) = Empty) Then
            Exit Sub
        End If
    Next intSub

    intSub = 1
    intFileNum = FreeFile

    Open "c:\BstFrndP" For Output As #intFileNum

    For intSub = 1 To 5
        Print #intFileNum, strFirstName(intSub)
    Next intSub

    Close #intFileNum
```

```
    intSub = 1
    intFileNum = FreeFile

    Open "c:\BstFrndW" For Output As #intFileNum

    For intSub = 1 To 5
        Write #intFileNum, strFirstName(intSub)
    Next intSub

    Close #intFileNum


    intSub = 1
    intFileNum = FreeFile

    Open "c:\BstFrndP" For Input As #intFileNum

    For intSub = 1 To 5
        Input #intFileNum, strFirstName(intSub)
        intMsg = MsgBox(strFirstName(intSub))
    Next intSub

    Close #intFileNum

End Sub
```

This block of code executes the entire program, with the exception of calling the procedure. The next code that needs to be added is the ***procedure call***.

Double-click the **Form** icon in the Project window. Your frmSequentialFile will open in the Form window editing area. Double-click on your form so that the code editing window opens. The Form object and Load procedure are listed in the drop-down list boxes at the top of the window. Type in the code as shown in Figure 7-3.

Your code is now complete.

**FIGURE 7-3**
Procedure call

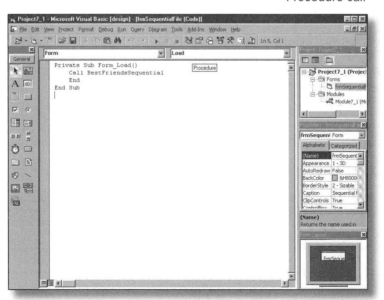

**Step 4: Save Your Project**

Save your project changes by clicking the **Save** button on the toolbar.

**Step 5: Run the Program**

Click the **Run** button on the toolbar to run your program, which should open in the middle of the screen. Notice that your form never shows. You will be prompted to enter the first names of your five best friends, one at a time, with an input box. The OK button will cause the loop to proceed. Once you have entered the names of your five best friends, the results display with five separate message boxes. If you select the Cancel button, the program will end.

The program executes the same as Project 6-1; however, behind the scenes your program creates two sequential files and reads the data back from one. This is a definite change from Project 6-1.

**Step 6: Review Your Code**

Now that your program has run successfully, answer the following questions. Review your answers with your classmates and teacher.

**1.** Explain the purpose of the following line of code:

```
Dim intFileNum As Integer
```

_____

_____

The intFileNum variable holds the file number that will be opened for writing and reading. You will see its use in the following code analysis.

We will skip reviewing the For loop that fills the array because you analyzed this block of code in the last lesson. The next block of code will "print" the contents of your array to the first sequential file.

```
intSub = 1
intFileNum = FreeFile

Open "c:\BstFrndP" For Output As #intFileNum

For intSub = 1 To 5
    Print #intFileNum, strFirstName(intSub)
Next intSub

Close #intFileNum
```

**2.** Explain why intSub is being reassigned the value of 1.

_____

_____

_____

_____

**3.** Explain the execution of the For loop.

_____

_____

**4.** Explain the Close statement.

_____

_____

The remainder of the code is new and will be explained line by line.

```
intFileNum = FreeFile
```

The **FreeFile** function finds the next free file number for you. In Visual Basic, files are referred to by number. You can either assign a number or simply use the FreeFile function to find the next free file number. In this case we assign the value of FreeFile to the intFileNum variable.

```
Open "c:\BstFrndP" For Output As #intFileNum
```

The **Open** statement opens a file for use. The **default mode** for the Open statement is **Random**. This means that data can be placed or retrieved from anywhere in the file. The other modes are **Append**, **Binary**, **Input**, and **Output**. Append adds data to the end of the file. Binary opens a file for binary level access. Input opens a file for reading. Output opens a file for writing.

The file BstFrndP is opened for Output, which means it will accept data in a sequential order, starting at the beginning of the file. The file itself will be created in the root directory of your hard drive and will be assigned the file number generated by the FreeFile function.

```
For intSub = 1 To 5
    Print #intFileNum, strFirstName(intSub)
Next intSub
```

The **Print #** statement will "print" records to the file number assigned through the FreeFile function. This print statement will write the first name variable to each record in the file. Now let's move on to the next block of code.

**5.** Compare this block of code to the one you just analyzed. Explain the differences between the two.

```
intSub = 1
intFileNum = FreeFile

Open "c:\BstFrndW" For Output As #intFileNum

For intSub = 1 To 5
    Write #intFileNum, strFirstName(intSub)
Next intSub

Close #intFileNum
```

_____

_____

_____

_____

_____

_____

Both the **Print #** statement and the **Write #** statement will write data to a file. The difference is that Write # **comma-delimits** the file, encloses all strings in quotation marks, encloses all date data within # signs, writes **Boolean** data as #TRUE# or #FALSE#, and sends null data and error codes to the file. Obviously the Write # statement is the better one to use.

**6.** The following block of code reads one of the files and uses message boxes to display the contents of the file. After comparing this block of code to the previous blocks, explain the block of code in the following space:

```
    intSub = 1
    intFileNum = FreeFile

    Open "c:\BstFrndP" For Input As #intFileNum

    For intSub = 1 To 5
        Input #intFileNum, strFirstName(intSub)
        intMsg = MsgBox(strFirstName(intSub))
    Next intSub

    Close #intFileNum

End Sub
```

_____

_____

_____

_____

_____

You should now have a pretty good idea of how to work with sequential access files.

## PROJECT 7-2 : Random Access File

In Lesson 2 you created a variety of forms for adding, modifying, deleting, and viewing/printing data. You were told that the functionality would be added later. In this project you will add the functionality to the Add A Record form created in Project 2-3. The information that is input by the user will be saved to a random access file.

To access your records in any order, you must have **fixed-length records**. By doing this VB will be able to calculate where the record is, or should be stored. VB takes the record number and multiplies it by the record size to find where it should be placed.

You will also use two new methods in getting your data into and out of the random access file. The **Put #** statement will write the appropriate record into your file, while the **Get #** statement will read the records from your file.

In this project you will not be using loops or arrays to handle your data. The data will be input into text boxes and then transferred into a *user-defined data type*, which is one that contains other existing data types, such as integers and strings. It is called a user-defined type because the programmer defines this type.

### Step 1: Start Your Compiler

Start your compiler if necessary.

### Step 2: Open Project 2-3

Open the **File** menu and click **Open Project**. In the Open Project dialog box, open your **Project 2-3** project from the Existing tab. Your VB environment should look like Figure 7-4.

**FIGURE 7-4**
Project 2-3

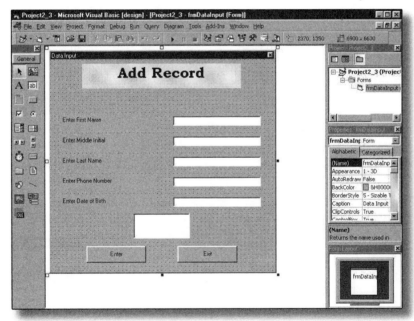

Immediately save your form as **DataInput7-2** and your project as **Project 7-2**. Rename your existing controls as follows:

| Control | Property | Value |
|---|---|---|
| Project | Name | Project7_2 |
| Form | Name | frmDataInput7_2 |
| | Caption | Data Input Project 7-2 |

Save your project once again by clicking the **Save** button on the toolbar.

## Step 3: Modify Your Form

Double-click your **Form** icon in the Project window to open the form in the Form window editing area. Delete the large text box at the bottom of your form. Resize the **Enter** and **Exit** commands buttons and then add a third command button of the same size. The new command button should read **Display Record**. Recaption the **Enter** command button as **Add Record**.

**1.** Write the names you give to your Add Record and Display Record command buttons in the following spaces:

| Control | Property | Value |
|---|---|---|
| Command1 | Name | _____ |
| | Caption | Add Record |
| Command2 | Name | _____ |
| | Caption | Display Record |

Your form should look like Figure 7-5.

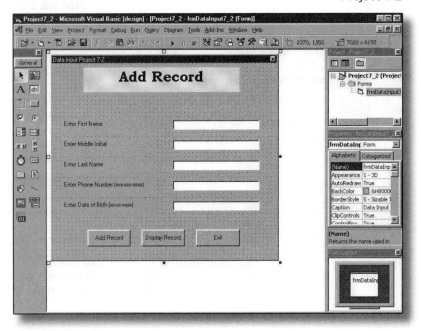

**FIGURE 7-5**
Project 7-2

Because you are dealing with a random access file, your records must be a fixed length. Before you code your form, you can help limit the amount of data input to each text box by setting the *MaxLength* property. The MaxLength property limits the number of characters that can be entered into a control. Set the maximum length of the first name to **20**, middle initial to **1**, last name to **20**, phone number to **12**, and date of birth to **10**.

**1.** Explain why you are setting the phone number property to 12 when most phone numbers have seven digits.

---

**2.** Explain why the date of birth will be set to a maximum length of 10 when the MM/DD/YY format usually has eight characters. (*Hint*: View Figure 7-5 and change your labels accordingly.)

_____

_____

### Step 4: Add Code at the Module Level

Declare your variables, including your user-defined type. The variables will be added at the *module level*. The variables that need to be added are shown in Figure 7-6.

Project 7-2 variables declaration

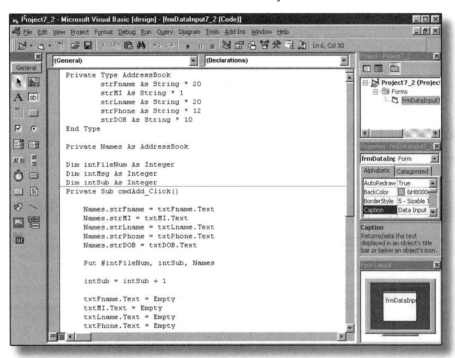

The word *General* is showing in the object list box, and the word *Declarations* is showing in the procedure list box. This is the module level. All user-defined types must be declared Private because they will be private to the form's module code. The other variables declared here can be used throughout the module.

The type AddressBook is your user-defined type. It consists of five text strings of varying length. Notice the "* 20." That is how length is assigned to a variable. You should also notice that the name of each string mimics the associated text box name, and the length of each string is the same as the MaxLength property. This maintains consistency throughout your program. The user-defined type ends with the End Type statement.

The next line, shown in the following box, actually creates an *instance* of your AddressBook type named Names. The first block of code defined what an AddressBook is; the preceding line actually created an AddressBook called Names. This will be the record structure you use to write to your file.

```
Private Names As AddressBook
```

**1.** Explain the following variable declarations:

```
Dim intFileNum As Integer
Dim intMsg As Integer
Dim intSub As Integer
```

_____

_____

_____

Now you can add code to your command buttons that will cause the program to execute when clicked.

### Step 5: Add Code to Your Command Buttons

The first button to which you will add code is the Add Record button. Double-click the **Add Record** button to open the code editing window. Then add the code that is shown in Figure 7-7.

**FIGURE 7-7**
Add Record button code

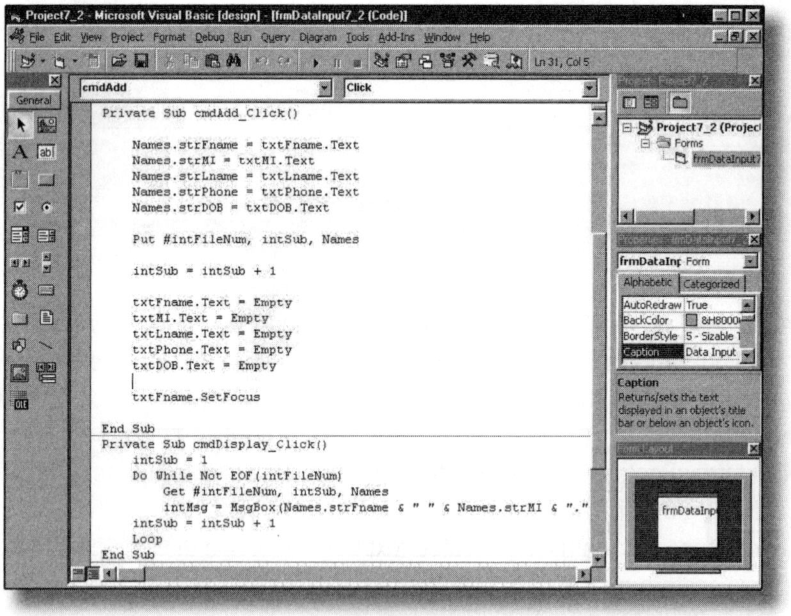

**1.** Explain the code added to the Add Record command button.

_____

_____

_____

Next you will add code to the Display Record button. Double-click the **Display Record** button to open the code editing window. Then add the code that is shown in the following box:

```
Private Sub cmdDisplay_Click()
    intSub = 1
    Do While Not EOF(intFileNum)
        Get #intFileNum, intSub, Names
        intMsg = MsgBox(Names.strFname & " " & Names.strMI &
                "." & " " & Names.strLname & "    " &
                Names.strPhone & "    " & Names.strDOB)
        intSub = intSub + 1
    Loop
End Sub
```

**2.** Explain the code added to the Display Record command button.

_____

_____

_____

_____

Last you will modify the existing block of code for the Exit button as shown in Figure 7-8. The Exit button code is highlighted in the figure.

**FIGURE 7-8**
Exit button code

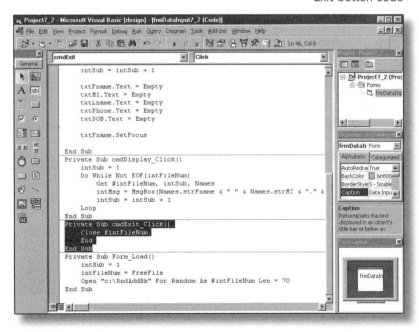

You still have one more section of code to add. This code will be attached to the form and will execute when the form opens, or loads. This code will be part of the **Form_Load** procedure, which is highlighted in Figure 7-9.

**FIGURE 7-9**
Form_Load procedure code

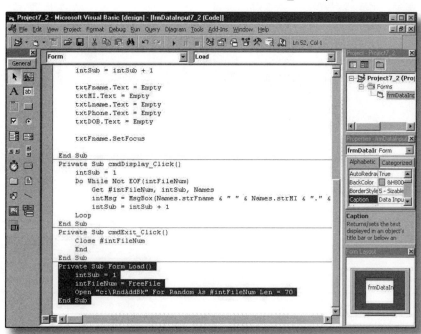

**3.** Explain the code added to the Form_Load procedure.

_____

_____

_____

_____

_____

_____

_____

_____

_____

_____

### Step 6: Save Your Project

Save your project changes by clicking the **Save** button on the toolbar.

### Step 7: Run Your Program

Click the **Run** button on the toolbar to run your program, which will start with the Add A Record form. You will enter the requested information in each text box and then click **Add Record** when

**164**

finished. Add as many records as you wish. When you are finished, you may either display the records you entered, or you may exit. Even if you exit, you will be able to display the records entered the last time you executed your program.

Your program takes the information from the text boxes, transfers it into the Names record, and then writes it to your random access file. After each record is input, the form is cleared, and *focus* is reset to the first text box.

When you click the Display Records button, your file is opened, and the records are read from the file. Each record is displayed to the screen using a message box. When the program reaches the end of the file, it terminates the display command. You choose when to terminate the entire program by clicking on the Exit button.

You now have a program that accesses random access files.

## P R O J E C T  7 - 3 : VB Data Control

This project deals with the **Data** control, which is the only VB database tool that comes with all versions. Therefore, to make sure everyone can experience interacting with an **Access database**, you will use this simple control. The Data control is simple and is always in the Toolbox. Those two reasons alone make this a useful tool.

You will create a form that reads from an Access database **table**, which is one data file within a database. The database you will use is the Northwind Traders database file (**Nwnd.mdb**) that comes with Visual Basic. Because the Data control is a **bound control**, it will allow you to bind other controls to the database, not just itself. You will use the Data and Label controls to view one of the tables from the Northwind Traders database.

(Check with your instructor for the location of the Northwind Traders database.)

### Step 1: Start Your Compiler

Start your compiler if necessary.

### Step 2: Create a New Project

Open the **File** menu, and click **New Project**. In the New Project dialog box, double-click the **Standard EXE** button.

### Step 3: Add Your Controls

For this project you will need six Label controls and one Data control. Resize your form and place your controls, as shown in Figure 7-10.

**FIGURE 7-10**
Project 7-3

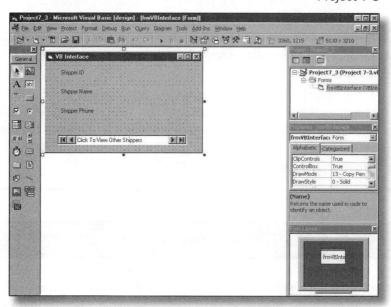

Change the appropriate properties for each control as follows:

| Control | Property | Value |
|---|---|---|
| Project | Name | Project7_3 |
| Form | Name | frmVBInterface |
| | Caption | VB Interface |
| Label1 | Name | lblShipID |
| | Caption | Shipper ID |
| Label2 | Name | lblShipName |
| | Caption | Shipper Name |
| Label3 | Name | lblShipPhone |
| | Caption | Shipper Phone |
| Label4 | Name | lblIDNum |
| | Alignment | Right justify |
| | Caption | None |
| | *DataField* | ShipperID |
| | *DataSource* | dtaDataControl |
| | Font | SettoBold |
| Label5 | Name | lblName |
| | Alignment | Right justify |
| | Caption | None |
| | DataField | CompanyName |
| | DataSource | dtaDataControl |
| | Font | SettoBold |
| Label6 | Name | lblPhone |
| | Alignment | Right justify |
| | Caption | None |
| | DataField | Phone |
| | DataSource | dtaDataControl |
| | Font | SettoBold |

**1 6 6**

| | | |
|---|---|---|
| DataControl1 | Name | dtaDataControl |
| | Caption | Click to View Other Shippers |
| | DatabaseName | Browse to path given by teacher |
| | RecordSource | Shippers |

Before you attempt to connect the Data control to the Northwind Traders database, make sure you know the correct location of the database. You can browse to the database by clicking in the DatabaseName property box. The same is true for the RecordSource property.

**Step 4: Save Your Project**

Save your project changes by clicking the **Save** button on the toolbar. In the Save As dialog box, save your new form as **frmVBInterface** and your project as **Project 7-3**.

**Step 5: Run the Program**

Click the **Run** button on the toolbar to run the program. Since the Data control is a bound control, there is no code to write. The functionality needed is built right in.

Your form opens and automatically displays the first record from the Shippers table. To view the next record, click the innermost right arrow button. To go to the last record, click the outermost right arrow button. The left arrow buttons work in the opposite manner, taking you back one record or taking you to the first record.

**Step 6: Review Your Code**

Now that your program has run successfully, answer the following questions. Review your answers with your classmates and teacher.

**1.** Which Data control property connects to the database?

______________________________________________

**2.** Which Data control property selects the database table to be used?

______________________________________________

**3.** Explain the purpose of the DataField and DataSource properties of the labels used to display the information.

______________________________________________

______________________________________________

**4.** Why does the information in labels 4, 5, and 6 display in bold?

______________________________________________

**5.** What control could be used in place of the labels if you wanted the user to change the data displayed?

______________________________________________

______________________________________________

You now have an example of how to interact with a Microsoft Access database.

# Summary

In this lesson you interfaced with multiple types of databases. You first created a sequential access file, which stores data in the order in which they are entered. They are accessed in the same way beginning with the first record. Even though this type of file is no longer widely used, the techniques apply to other file types. You learned how to create two different types of files using two different commands, one more robust than the other.

You moved on to random access files, which can be written to, or retrieved from, anywhere in the file. The key to manipulating this type of file is to have the records all the same length. You learned how to declare variables with set lengths and to use the MaxLength property to enforce the input limits. You also learned two new commands to enter data into specific places in the file.

You then interacted with a sample Microsoft Access database. The Data control, the only database tool available with all versions of VB, bound the Northwind Traders database to the controls on your form. Because the Data control is a bound control, no additional code was necessary. Once your form is designed and the controls are bound, the interface works automatically when the program is run.

The projects you created were complex and covered a lot of territory and introduced very important topics for use throughout your programming career. Use these as a stepping stone to more intricate and complex interactions with databases.

## LESSON 7 REVIEW QUESTIONS

### SHORT ANSWER

**Define the following in the space provided.**

1. Random access

2. Append

3. Microsoft Access database

4. Sequential files

5. Procedure call

6. Boolean

7. Open

_____

_____

8. Comma-delimited

_____

9. Fixed-length records

_____

_____

10. Put #

_____

11. Get #

_____

_____

12. User-defined data type

_____

_____

_____

13. MaxLength property

_____

_____

14. Module level

_____

_____

_____

15. Instance

_____

_____

_____

16. Focus

_____

_____

17. Form_Load procedure

_____

_____

**18.** Data control

_____

_____

**19.** Table

_____

**20.** DatabaseName property

_____

**21.** RecordSource property

_____

**22.** DataSource property

_____

**23.** DataField property

_____

## WRITTEN QUESTIONS

**Write your answers to the following questions in the space provided.**

**1.** Explain the difference between the Print # and the Write # statements.

_____

_____

**2.** Explain why the Write # statement is the more robust.

_____

_____

_____

**3.** Explain the FreeFile function.

_____

_____

_____

**4.** List and explain the five modes of the Open statement.

_____

_____

_____

_____

_____

_____

_____

**5.** Explain the term *bound control*.

_____

_____

**6.** Explain why no code is needed for the Data control.

_____

**7.** Explain the advantages of using the Data control.

_____

**8.** Declare a user-defined data type of your choice in the following space:

_____

_____

_____

_____

_____

## TESTING YOUR SKILLS

### APPLICATION 7-1

In Project 7-2 you coded a program that created a random access file. Your random access file contained a person's first name, middle initial, last name, phone number, and date of birth. Even though this file was created in a random access format with the appropriate random access commands, the data were processed sequentially. In this application you will make your file access truly random access.

**1.** Open your **Project 7-2**. Save your form as **DataInputApp7-1**, and then save your project as **App7-1**.

**2.** Add a label and text box to your form. The label will identify the text box as the input area for a record number. Name your label and text box accordingly. Place the proper caption on the label.

**3.** Add an additional data type to the AddressBook declaration that corresponds to the record number text box. You will now explicitly keep track of each record number entered. The entry of the data will now be random.

**4.** The record number input by the user will be assigned to the record number member of the user-defined data type. The record number input by the user will also be assigned to the intSub variable that is used to place the data in a specific record number.

5. Save your project.

6. Run your project to test it. Then debug it if necessary. Run it again.

## APPLICATION 7-2

In Project 7-3 you used the Data control to access the sample Northwind Traders database. Every control you used besides the Data control was a Label control. Using the Label controls made your access read only. In this application you will access another database and make changes to it.

1. Create a new project with one form. Save the form as **AccessChange** and the project as **App7-2**.

2. Design your form so it is similar to the one used in Project 7-3. In this application you will need five Label controls, five TextBox controls, and one Data control.

3. You will be binding your controls to an Access database named **Names.mdb**, which is available with the Student Data & Resources Files accompanying this course. Because you are using bound controls, no additional code is necessary.

4. The TextBox controls will be used to display the contents of the database fields. By using text boxes instead of labels, your users will be able to modify the data contained in the Names database.

5. Save your project.

6. Run your project to test it. Then debug it if necessary. Run it again.

## CRITICAL THINKING

Estimated Time: 10 hours

1. Using Project 7-2 as an example, add functionality to the other menu forms from Lesson 2.

2. Project 7-2 created a random access file that stores the records you enter. Use this file as the database for your other forms.

3. Add the necessary code to make the Modify A Record, Delete A Record, and View/Print A Record functional.

# OBJECT LINKING AND EMBEDDING

## OBJECTIVES

**Upon completion of this lesson, you should be able to:**

■ Understand the difference between linking and embedding.

■ Demonstrate the difference between linking and embedding.

■ Embed an object in your application.

■ Link to an object from your application.

*Estimated Time: 5 hours*

## *Introduction*

In this lesson you will move from developing self-contained applications to developing applications that contain other applications and objects or are contained by other applications and objects. This is called *Object Linking and Embedding,* or *OLE*.

Application development is moving away from standalone applications into distributed applications. This means that all programs will have the option of interacting with other computers in some way. It could be as simple as connecting your computer game to other players over a network or the Internet, or it could be as complicated as providing secure transactions to customers who wish to use their credit card to purchase items over the Internet.

*COM*, the *Component Object Model* and the basis for OLE, is the standard by which software components can use each other. This is a restatement of the definition of OLE. *DCOM*, the *Distributed Component Object Model*, can be described as network OLE. This provides the same ability to use other software components, but it also extends the use over a network. Separate pieces of the same program can exist and operate on multiple computer systems. The programming model for COM and DCOM is identical to *ActiveX*. Therefore, OLE can be referred to as "early ActiveX." You will be introduced to ActiveX in Lesson 9.

This lesson is quick and simple, but it provides you with an important basis for understanding ActiveX. The projects you create in this lesson will form a basis for everything you do in the next two lessons. So work hard and have fun!

This lesson focuses on the following:

■ **Understanding and explaining the difference between linking and embedding.** The differences are slight but important because they provide the user with different versions of the same thing.

- **Embedding an object in your application.** You will embed an object in your application and then interact with it to explore the possibilities and limitations.

- **Linking to an object from your application.** You will link to an object from your application and then interact with it to explore the possibilities and limitations. You will also compare the differences between embedding and linking.

## PROJECT 8-1 : Bitmap Image Embedding  (B)

You will insert, or *embed*, a bitmap image into your form in this project, which means that a copy of the object is actually what is contained in your OLE control. If you embed an existing object, any changes to that object through other applications will not be reflected in your application. Think of this as inserting a read-only object into your program. The user can see it and use it but cannot change the original.

When you access your object, you can take advantage of using the menus and commands of its *parent application*. This is known as *in-place activation*. This gives you the ability to edit your object using the controls with which it was created. However, you may not have all the controls available that belong to the parent application. You will also notice that you will not have the ability to save your object as you would save a regular file. You will need to program your own save method.

Even though you will face some limitations, the process you are using will prove to be invaluable throughout your programming career. (Check the file path in the code. Check with your instructor to make sure this is where your files should be created.)

### Step 1: Start Your Compiler

Start your compiler if it is not already running.

### Step 2: Create a New Project

Open the **File** menu and click **New Project**. In the New Project window, double-click the **Standard EXE** button.

### Step 3: Add Your Controls

For this project you will need one OLE control and two Command Button controls. Resize your form and place your controls as shown in Figure 8-1. Make the OLE control the last control that you add to your form. You will do this in Step 4.

**FIGURE 8-1**
Placing controls

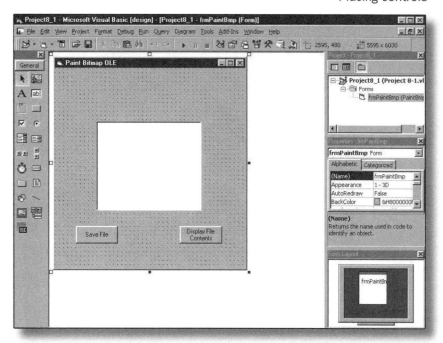

Change the appropriate properties for each control as follows:

| Control | Property | Value |
|---------|----------|-------|
| Project | Name | Project8_1 |
| Form | Name | frmPaintBmp |
| | Caption | Paint Bitmap OLE |
| Command1 | Name | cmdSave |
| | Caption | Save File |
| Command2 | Name | cmdDisplay |
| | Caption | Display File Contents |
| OLE1 | Name | olePaintBmp |
| | Height | 2500 |
| | Left | 1200 |
| | SizeMode | 1-Stretch |
| | Top | 1500 |

### Step 4: Insert (Embed) Your Bitmap Image

Double-click the **OLE control** to add it to your form. When it appears on the form, wait for the Insert Object dialog box to open to prompt you for the type of object you would like to insert. This dialog box is shown in Figure 8-2.

FIGURE 8-2
Insert Object dialog box

Leave the **Bitmap Image** selection highlighted and the **Create New** option selected. Click the **OK** button, and in a few seconds you will see scrollbars appear in your OLE control. When you click on anything else, the scrollbars will disappear. Do not worry about it. They will be back when you run your program.

Return to the control properties shown earlier and modify the values for your OLE control.

### Step 5: Save Your Project

Save your project by clicking the **Save** button on the toolbar. Save your new form as **PaintBmp** and your project as **Project 8-1**.

### Step 6: Add Code to Your Controls

Add the code shown in Figure 8-3 to the appropriate command button.

Save your program before continuing.

**FIGURE 8-3**
Command button code

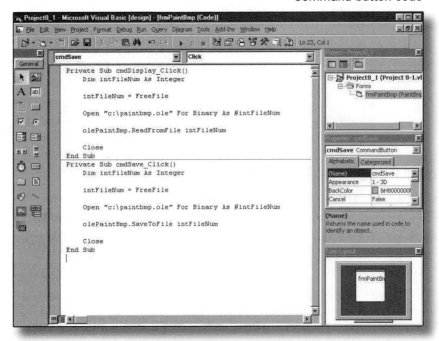

### Step 7: Run the Program

Click the **Run** button on the toolbar to run your program. Your program should open in the middle of the screen. Your OLE container will be empty. To activate the embedded object, double-click the **OLE** control. The OLE property that oversees this method is the ***AutoActivate*** property. The default is 2-Double-Click, which is the setting for this project.

When your embedded object opens, you will see a blank drawing area with two scrollbars. You will also notice that you have a menu that belongs to the Paint program, which is the bitmap's parent application. Take a few moments to explore the menu. Notice that the options listed on the menu are not complete. For example, there are no options for saving or opening files. To save your drawings, you need to add code to the Save File command button, which you did.

Take a few minutes to draw something in the drawing area. Use the menu options available to you. When you are finished, click the **Save File** command button. Notice that the picture you drew now displays in the OLE container, and the scrollbars have disappeared. This is the representation of the saved file that is being displayed.

Obviously, if you click on the Display File Contents button, the file you just saved will display. BUT you still need to double-click on the OLE control to activate it! To test the Display File Contents button, close your application and then reopen it. When it reopens, double-click the **OLE** control and *then* click the **Display** command button. This way you will be assured of opening the most recently saved file if you continue to make changes.

Make sure you experiment with the Save and Display buttons in order to become familiar with the way they work.

### Step 8: Review Your Code

Now that your program has run successfully, answer the following questions. Review your answers with your classmates and teacher.

**1.** Explain the following line of code:

```
Open "c:\paintbmp.ole" For Binary As #intFileNum
```

_____

_____

**2.** Explain the following line of code:

```
olePaintBmp.ReadFromFile intFileNum
```

_____

**3.** Explain the following line of code:

```
olePaintBmp.SaveToFile intFileNum
```

_____

_____

You are now able to embed objects in your forms.

In this project you will **embed** and **link** two existing files. The methods for embedding a file and linking files is a little different. Primarily, the parent application will perform differently between the execution of the embedded file and the linked file. When you link files, the full parent application will be available to you when you activate the OLE control. The link is actually a "pointer" to the original file contained in the OLE control. Therefore, you are working with the original file, instead of a static copy of it, as is the case when you embed an object.

This project also gives you practice working with multiple forms once again. You will create a menu form that will offer selections between the first form you create for this project and the form from Project 8-1. And then you will add the form from Project 8-1 to this project.

### Step 1: Start Your Compiler

Start your compiler if necessary.

### Step 2: Create a New Project

Open the **File** menu and click **New Project**. In the New Project window, double-click the **Standard EXE** button.

### Step 3: Add Your Controls

For this project you will need two OLE controls and two Label controls. Resize your form and place your controls as shown in Figure 8-4. Make your OLE controls the last controls that you add to your form. You will do this in Step 4.

**FIGURE 8-4**
Project 8-2

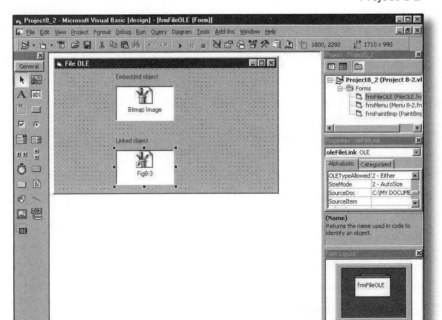

Change the appropriate properties for each control as follows;

| Control | Property | Value |
|---|---|---|
| Project | Name | Project8_2 |
| Form | Name | frmFileOLE |
| | Caption | File OLE |
| Label1 | Name | lblEmbed |
| | Caption | Embedded object |
| Label2 | Name | lblLink |
| | Caption | Linked object |
| OLE1 | Name | oleFileEmbed |
| | SizeMode | 2-AutoSize |
| OLE2 | Name | oleFileLink |
| | SizeMode | 2-AutoSize |

### Step 4: Embed Your Bitmap Image

Double-click your **OLE** control to add the first control to your form. When the Insert Object dialog box opens (it may take a bit longer than you expect), click the **Create from File** option button. The Insert Object dialog box changes to look like that shown in Figure 8-5.

**FIGURE 8-5**
Insert Object dialog box—Create from File

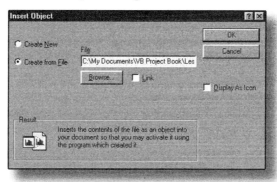

Click the **Browse** button to search for the **Fig8-2.bmp** file, stored in the Student Data & Resources files accompanying this course. When you locate the file, double-click its icon. This will return you to the Insert Object dialog box. Click the **Display As Icon** check box. Do *not* choose any other option. Click the **OK** button. An icon will appear in your OLE control, and the OLE control will resize itself.

Return to the control properties shown earlier and modify the values for your OLE control.

Double-click the **OLE** control again to add a second OLE control to your form. When the Insert Object dialog box appears, click the **Create from File** option button again.

Click the **Browse** button to search for the **Fig8-3.bmp** file, stored in the Student Data & Resources files accompanying this course. When you locate the file, double-click its icon. This will return you to the Insert Object dialog box. Click the **Display As Icon** check box. Also click the **Link** check box. Click **OK**. An icon will appear in your OLE control, and the OLE control will resize itself.

Return to the control properties shown earlier and modify the values for your second OLE control.

## Step 5: Save Your Project

Save your project by clicking the **Save** button on the toolbar. Save your new form as **FileOLE** and your project as **Project 8-2**.

## Step 6: Run the Program

Click the **Run** button on the toolbar to run your program, which should open in the middle of the screen. Your OLE container will not be empty this time. Because you selected Display As Icon in the Insert Object dialog box, both objects are displayed by using icons of the file type.

To activate the embedded object, double-click the **embedded OLE** control. The OLE property that oversees this method is the AutoActivate property. The default is 2-Double-Click for this project. When your embedded object opens, you will see the Paint environment. Take a few moments to explore the menus. Notice that the options listed on the menu are not complete. For example, there are no options for saving or opening files. However, you do have the Save As option. This is supposed to protect your original file by suggesting that you should save it with another filename. This could be dangerous because a user can save over the same file name if he or she knows it. Take a few minutes to modify this bitmap file and save it under a name of your choice. Use the menu options available to you.

To activate the linked object, double-click the **linked OLE** control. When this object opens, it is the original object, *not* a copy. Notice when you explore your menu choices under this option that the full menu choices are there. Take a few minutes to modify this bitmap file and save it under a name of your choice. Use the menu options available to you.

## Step 7: Create a Menu Form

Add a new form to this project. Add three command buttons. One will show the form you just completed, another will show the form from Project 8-1, and the third will exit the program. Figure 8-6 displays a sample menu.

**FIGURE 8-6**
Sample menu form

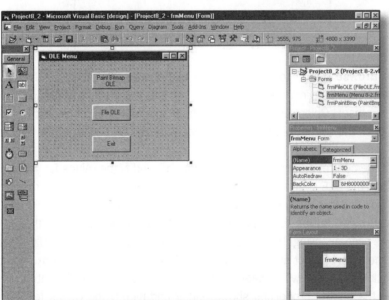

1. Once you lay out your form, make sure you modify the following properties. Write the values you use in the appropriate blanks:

| Control | Property | Value |
|---|---|---|
| Project | Name | Project8_2 |
| Form | Name | _____ |
|  | Caption | _____ |
| Command1 | Name | _____ |
|  | Caption | _____ |
| Command2 | Name | _____ |
|  | Caption | _____ |
| Command3 | Name | _____ |
|  | Caption | _____ |

2. Now you need to add code to your command buttons. Write your code in the space provided:

Command1

_____

_____

_____

Command2

_____

_____

_____

Command3

_____

_____

_____

3. You now need to make the menu form your startup object. Explain how you make a form a startup object for a project.

_____

_____

4. You now need to add the **PaintBmp** form from Project 8-1 to this project. Add the form to this project. Explain how you add an existing form to a project.

_____

_____

_____

After completing the four steps above, save your project, and then run it. If it does not run correctly, debug it, and then run it again.

You are now able to embed and link objects in your forms.

# Summary

This lesson introduced you to OLE, which is also known as early ActiveX. It will form the basis for everything you do in the remainder of this text. OLE is the sharing of software components. This means that one application can contain one or many objects that belong to other applications.

You were also introduced to the terms COM and DCOM. COM is the basis upon which OLE is built. DCOM is the network version of COM. The importance of this is that most applications today are developed to run on multiple computers. One part will run on the client machine, another on an intermediary machine, and a third part usually on a database server. Remember our earlier discussions about the emphasis on databases and data storage/retrieval. OLE is the building block that begins to bring all this together.

You embedded and linked objects in this lesson's projects. You learned that the process is similar regardless of the objects being used. The next two lessons will build upon these basic concepts.

## LESSON 8 REVIEW QUESTIONS

### SHORT ANSWER

**Define the following in the space provided.**

1. OLE

2. COM

3. DCOM

4. Embed

5. Link

6. Parent application

7. In-Place Activation

_____

_____

8. OLE control

_____

_____

9. SizeMode property

_____

10. AutoActivate property

_____

## WRITTEN QUESTIONS

**Write your answers to the following questions in the space provided.**

1. Explain how to embed a new object.

_____

_____

_____

_____

2. Explain how to embed an existing object.

_____

_____

_____

_____

3. Explain how to link an object.

_____

_____

_____

4. Explain the difference between linking and embedding.

_____

_____

5. Explain how to display your embedded or linked object as an icon.

_____

6. Explain the difference between using a new embedded object and an existing embedded object.

_____

_____

_____

_____

7. Explain why you needed to save your bitmap in Project 8-1, but you received full functionality with the objects in Project 8-2.

_____

_____

_____

8. Explain the difference between COM and DCOM.

_____

_____

9. Explain the use of the SizeMode property.

_____

_____

10. Explain the use of the AutoActivate property.

_____

_____

## TESTING YOUR SKILLS

Creating OLE objects is fairly simple. Instead of having you simply repeat the same steps in a number of end-of-lesson applications, you will apply your knowledge and skills in the following Critical Thinking problem.

## CRITICAL THINKING

 Estimated Time: 5 hours

1. Create a new project and attempt to embed and link to one of your existing projects. Explain what happens in each case. How might you solve the problems if you encounter any?

2. Create a new project and attempt to embed and link to one of the data files you created with one of your projects. Explain what happens in each case. How might you solve the problems if you encounter any?

3. Create an .exe file for one of your projects, or select a project that you have already made into an executable file. Create a new project and attempt to embed and link to your executable file. Explain what happens in each case. How might you solve the problems if you encounter any?

SCANS

# ACTIVEX

## OBJECTIVES

**Upon completion of this lesson, you should be able to:**

- Explain ActiveX, ActiveX automation, and ActiveX controls.

- Use an existing ActiveX control in an application.

- Integrate ActiveX automation into an application.

- Create your own ActiveX control.

- Integrate your ActiveX control in an application.

🕐 **Estimated Time: 10 hours**

## *Introduction*

Welcome to *ActiveX*. As you learned in Lesson 8, ActiveX, OLE, COM, and DCOM are related. In this lesson we focus on ActiveX.

ActiveX refers to custom-designed controls that can be created by anyone. ActiveX began as add-in controls that extended what programmers could do in VB. Because these extended controls were not compatible with anything except VB and because they became extremely popular, Microsoft redesigned them so that they could be used with multiple applications, programming languages, and Internet browsers. When installed, VB adds several ActiveX components to your system. You can add these controls to your projects through the *Components dialog box* and then use them just like any of the other common controls.

You can also *automate* controls between applications that are registered as ActiveX applications in your system's *registry*. You can open an application within your VB application, use its controls and commands, and then embed the resulting file in your application's form—all without directly opening the application. You need to be aware that each ActiveX application contains its own *automation language*. To become familiar with the capabilities of various ActiveX applications, search their online Help system for their object hierarchy. This will provide you with the available objects from that application with which you can interface.

VB allows you to create your own ActiveX controls. You can create a control that is a *subclass* of an existing control, or you can subclass a control from multiple other controls, or you can create a control from scratch. A subclass is a control that *inherits* properties from a higher class. A command button is an example of a class. Until you add it to a form and customize it to your needs, it is only a "blueprint" or a description of a command button. This generic command button contains properties, events, and methods. If you were to add additional, different properties, events, or methods to the command button, you would be making a subclass. This subclass would contain everything included in the higher class *and* the items you added. That's why the term ***inheritance*** is used—the subclass "inherits" the properties, events, and methods from the higher class.

You can create controls that fit your needs. And if they fit the needs of many other users, you then have a product that you can sell. Many companies do nothing but write and sell custom ActiveX controls. You will only scratch the surface of ActiveX in this lesson. It is a powerful and complex topic. However, you will have the basic ActiveX tools you need to build upon as you move into your programming career.

This lesson will focus on the following:

■ **Explaining ActiveX, ActiveX automation, and ActiveX controls.** You will be able to explain the concept of ActiveX and its various uses.

■ **Using an existing ActiveX control in an application.** You will use an existing ActiveX control in an application. You will see how the various properties can be manipulated just like any other VB control.

■ **Integrating ActiveX automation into an application.** You will use ActiveX automation to allow a user to use the commands and properties of another ActiveX application from within your VB application.

■ **Creating your own ActiveX control and integrating it in an application.** You will create an ActiveX control that is a subclass of an existing control. In the end-of-lesson applications, you will use your ActiveX control in one of your programs.

## PROJECT 9-1: The Multimedia Control  (B)

You will add the ***Microsoft Multimedia Control (MMC)*** to your Toolbox and then use it in this project. The MMC allows you to embed objects that represent the following devices:

Audio CD player (CDAudio)

Digital Audio Tape player (DAT)

Wave Player (WaveAudio)

Digital Video files (DigitalVideo)

Overlay (Overlay)

Scanner (Scanner)

Videotape player and recorder (Vcr)

Videodisc player (Videodisc)

You will use the MMC to create a Wave Player. This device will play ***wave*** (.wav) files. Because Windows comes with multiple wave files, you will have multiple sound files with which to experiment.

 **HOT TIP**

Check the file path in the MMC FileName property for access to the wave file. Check with your instructor to make sure this is where your files are stored.

**186**

### Step 1: Start Your Compiler

Start your compiler if it is not already running.

### Step 2: Create a New Project

Open the **File** menu and click **New Project**. When the New Project window appears, double-click the **Standard EXE** button.

### Step 3: Add the Microsoft Multimedia Control

All ActiveX controls available on your system can be found by opening the **Project** menu and then selecting **Components**. The Components dialog box will appear. Scroll down the list box until you find the **Microsoft Multimedia Control**. Select it by clicking the check box as shown in Figure 9-1, and then click **OK**. The MMC will appear in your Toolbox.

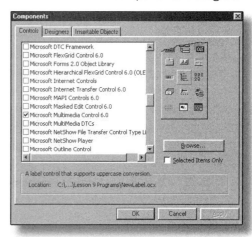

**FIGURE 9-1**
Components dialog box

### Step 4: Add the MMC to Your Form

Double-click the **MMC** in your Toolbox to add it to your form. This control looks similar to the controls found on a typical audio CD or VCR. Remember this when designing your own controls from scratch—make the controls similar to the device they are mimicking.

Your form should look like Figure 9-2.

**FIGURE 9-2**
MMC

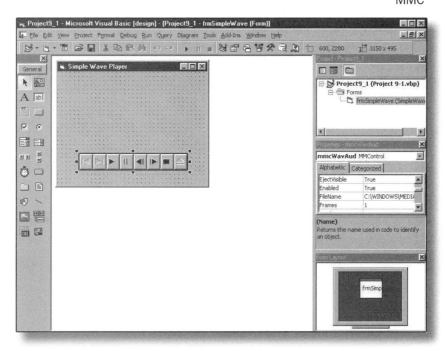

**187**

### Step 5: Modify Your Control Properties

You now need to modify your project, form, and MMC. Change the properties as shown:

| Control | Property | Value |
| --- | --- | --- |
| Project | Name | Project9_1 |
| Form | Name | frmSimpleWave |
| | Caption | Simple Wave Player |
| MMControl1 | Name | mmcWavAud |
| | DeviceType | WaveAudio |
| | FileName | Applause.wav |
| | Custom | See next paragraph |

You will also need to modify the control button properties that belong to the MMC. Click the **Custom** property, and then click the ellipse that appears. A Property Pages dialog box appears. Click the **Controls** tab. The default settings for the controls are shown in Figure 9-3.

You will need to modify the defaults to those shown in Figure 9-4.

The changes to the Controls options will cause the Step, Back, Pause, Play, and Stop controls to be enabled. The Record button will disappear. Your MMC is now ready to be used.

**FIGURE 9-3**
MMC Property Pages dialog box
—Controls tab defaults

**FIGURE 9-4**
Modifying Controls tab settings

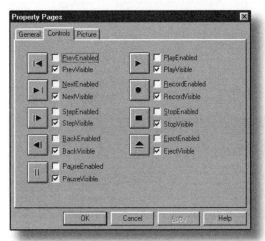

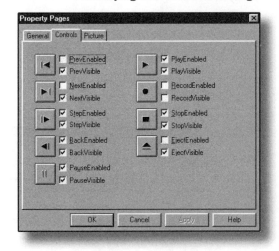

### Step 6: Add Code to Your Form

You now need to add two blocks of code to your form. Your Wave Player will be opened when the form loads, and it will be closed when the form unloads. Add the blocks of code shown in Figure 9-5 to your form load and form unload events.

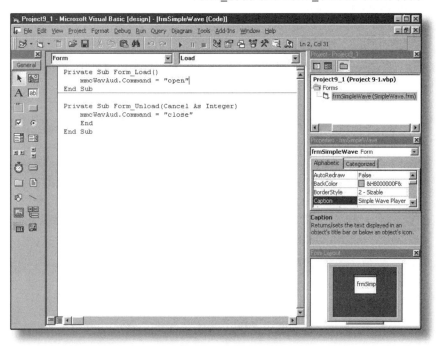

**FIGURE 9-5**
Form_Load and Form_Unload event code

## Step 7: Save Your Project

Save your project changes by clicking the **Save** button on the toolbar. Save the form as **SimpleWave** and the project as **Project 9-1**.

## Step 8: Run the Program

Click the **Run** button on the toolbar to run the program. The form will contain one control—the MMC. Test the form by clicking the proper control buttons. Notice that if you wish to replay the wave file, you will need to click the **Back** button before playing it again. Also notice that the buttons not enabled are dimmed and that the Record button is not even shown.

You have now added and used an existing ActiveX control.

---

## P R O J E C T   9 - 2 : ActiveX Automation

You will create an application that prompts a user for input and then creates a spreadsheet file with the information. Your application will use ActiveX automation to interact with Microsoft Excel's capabilities to create the spreadsheet for the user.

Automation is the process of one application's capabilities being used by another application. Remember that you are limited to using automation only for those applications that are registered as ActiveX in your system's registry. Your application will also save your spreadsheet file and workbook to disk. Make sure you check with your instructor for the correct path to where your files should be created.

## Step 1: Start Your Compiler

Start your compiler if necessary.

## Step 2: Create a New Project

Open the **File** menu and click **New Project**. When the New Project window appears, double-click the **Standard EXE** button.

## Step 3: Modify Your Form

Modify your form to look like the input form displayed in Figure 9-6.

**FIGURE 9-6**
Project 9-2 input form

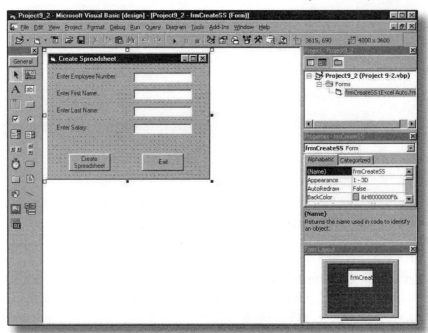

1. Write the names you give to your controls in the spaces provided:

| Control | Property | Value |
|---|---|---|
| Project | Name | _____ |
| Form | Name | _____ |
| | Caption | _____ |
| Label1 | Name | _____ |
| | Caption | _____ |
| Label2 | Name | _____ |
| | Caption | _____ |
| Label3 | Name | _____ |
| | Caption | _____ |
| Label4 | Name | _____ |
| | Caption | _____ |

| Text1 | Name | _____ |
| | Alignment | _____ |
| | TabIndex | _____ |
| | Text | _____ |
| Text2 | Name | _____ |
| | Alignment | _____ |
| | TabIndex | _____ |
| | Text | _____ |
| Text3 | Name | _____ |
| | Alignment | _____ |
| | TabIndex | _____ |
| | Text | _____ |
| Text4 | Name | _____ |
| | Alignment | _____ |
| | TabIndex | _____ |
| | Text | _____ |
| Command1 | Name | _____ |
| | Caption | _____ |
| | TabIndex | _____ |
| Command2 | Name | _____ |
| | Caption | _____ |
| | TabIndex | _____ |

## Step 4: Add Code to the Form and Command Buttons

First you will declare your variables, which will be added at the **module level**. The variables that need to be added are shown in Figure 9-7.

**FIGURE 9-7**
Project 9-2 variables declaration

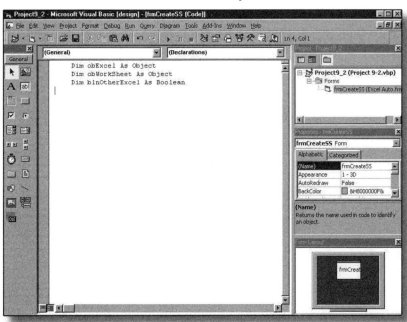

Now you can add code to your command buttons that will cause the program to execute when clicked or to exit, depending on the choice the user makes. The code for the Create Spreadsheet command button is as follows. If your control names are different from those provided, change the code to reflect the control names you are using.

```
Private Sub cmdCreate_Click()
    On Error Resume Next

    Set obExcel = GetObject(, "Excel.application")

    If Err.Number <> 0 Then
        Set obExcel = CreateObject("Excel.application")
        blnOtherExcel = False
    Else
        blnOtherExcel = True
    End If

    obExcel.Workbooks.Add

    Set obWorkSheet = obExcel.ActiveSheet

    obWorkSheet.Cells(1, 1).Value = "Employee Number"
    obWorkSheet.Cells(1, 2).Value = "First Name"
    obWorkSheet.Cells(1, 3).Value = "Last Name"
    obWorkSheet.Cells(1, 4).Value = "Salary"
    obWorkSheet.Cells(2, 1).Value = txtEmpNum.Text
    obWorkSheet.Cells(2, 2).Value = txtFName.Text
    obWorkSheet.Cells(2, 3).Value = txtLName.Text
    obWorkSheet.Cells(2, 4).Value = Val(txtSalary.Text)

    obWorkSheet.Cells(2, 4).Select
    obExcel.Selection.NumberFormat = "$##,###.##"

    obExcel.Save ("c:\VBExcel.xls")

    obExcel.ActiveWorkBook.Close False

    If Not (blnOtherExcel) Then
        obExcel.Quit
    End If

    txtEmpNum.Text = Empty
    txtFName.Text = Empty
    txtLName.Text = Empty
    txtSalary.Text = Empty
    txtEmpNum.SetFocus
End Sub
```

The code for the Exit button is highlighted in Figure 9-8.

**FIGURE 9-8**
Project 9-2 Exit command button code

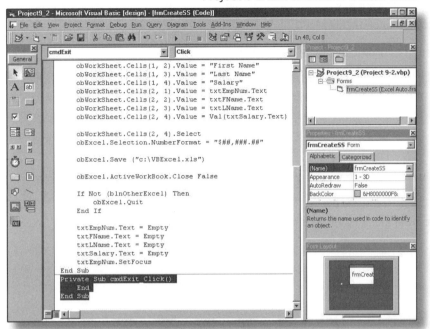

### Step 5: Save Your Project

Save your project changes by clicking the **Save** button on the toolbar. Save the form as **Excel Auto** and the project as **Project 9-2**.

### Step 6: Run Your Program

Click the **Run** button on the toolbar to run the program. Your program will start with your input form. Once you input the necessary information, you should click the **Create Spreadsheet** command button. When this button is clicked, "behind-the-scenes" automation takes place.

The first time your application is executed, you will be prompted to save the workbook that is being created. Save the workbook as **VBExcel Book1** in the location specified by your instructor. The completed spreadsheet will appear momentarily before returning you to the input form. If you run this application a second time, the spreadsheet file will be overwritten. A warning message will display asking whether you would like to overwrite the file. Each time you run the program, you will encounter the Save As dialog box for the workbook file.

When you return to the input form, the text boxes will all appear empty, and the first text box will have the focus. Your application is set up to allow you to expand the program to accept more than one row of spreadsheet information. Right now you can input only one row of information.

In order to check the file that was created, open Excel (or a spreadsheet program that can read .xls files) and then open the spreadsheet file created with this project.

**Step 7: Review Your Code**

Now that your program has run successfully, answer the following questions. Review your answers with your classmates and teacher.

**1.** Explain the following variable declarations.

```
Dim obExcel As Object
Dim obWorkSheet As Object
Dim blnOtherExcel As Boolean
```

_____

_____

_____

**2.** Explain the following block of code:

```
On Error Resume Next

Set obExcel = GetObject(, "Excel.application")

If Err.Number <> 0 Then
    Set obExcel = CreateObject("Excel.application")
    blnOtherExcel = False
Else
    blnOtherExcel = True
End If
```

_____

_____

_____

_____

_____

**3.** Explain the following block of code:

```
obExcel.Workbooks.Add

Set obWorkSheet = obExcel.ActiveSheet

obWorkSheet.Cells(1, 1).Value = "Employee Number"
obWorkSheet.Cells(1, 2).Value = "First Name"
obWorkSheet.Cells(1, 3).Value = "Last Name"
obWorkSheet.Cells(1, 4).Value = "Salary"
obWorkSheet.Cells(2, 1).Value = txtEmpNum.Text
obWorkSheet.Cells(2, 2).Value = txtFName.Text
obWorkSheet.Cells(2, 3).Value = txtLName.Text
obWorkSheet.Cells(2, 4).Value = Val(txtSalary.Text)

obWorkSheet.Cells(2, 4).Select
obExcel.Selection.NumberFormat = "$##,###.##"

obExcel.Save ("c:\VBExcel.xls")
```

**194**

**4.** Explain the following block of code:

```
obExcel.ActiveWorkBook.Close False

If Not (blnOtherExcel) Then
    obExcel.Quit
End If
```

**5.** Explain the following block of code.

```
txtEmpNum.Text = Empty
txtFName.Text = Empty
txtLName.Text = Empty
txtSalary.Text = Empty
txtEmpNum.SetFocus
```

You are now able to perform a simple ActiveX automation between applications.

## PROJECT 9 - 3 : ActiveX User-Defined Control

There are many companies in the computer industry earning lots of money by creating ActiveX controls and selling them to programmers. In this project you create your own ActiveX control—a modified Label control. You will add a property to your Label control that will allow the user to change the Caption contents to uppercase.

There are three ways to create new ActiveX controls: subclass a simple control, subclass multiple controls, or create your own from scratch. You will subclass a simple control in this project. You will start with an existing Label control and modify it by adding a new property. You can add multiple properties, events, and methods if you desire, but this project will be kept simple. Once you gain more experience, you may want to try creating a new control from multiple controls or create a control from scratch.

You will also find that this project is more complicated than the others. Instead of starting with a new project, you will be required to start with the creation of an ActiveX Control. Once your ActiveX control is created, you will add it to a project in order to test it. In the end-of-lesson applications you will actually create a project that uses your new control.

## Step 1: Start Your Compiler

Start your compiler if necessary.

## Step 2: New ActiveX Control Preliminaries

**FIGURE 9-9**
ActiveX Control icon

Open the **File** menu and click **New Project**. When the New Project window appears, double-click the **ActiveX Control** icon as shown in Figure 9-9.

This causes a new project to open; however, this new project contains a form without a title bar. This form is actually a holder that will contain your new ActiveX control. The default name of this form is **UserControl1**, not Form1. Figure 9-10 shows the default environment window with UserControl1.

**FIGURE 9-10**
UserControl1

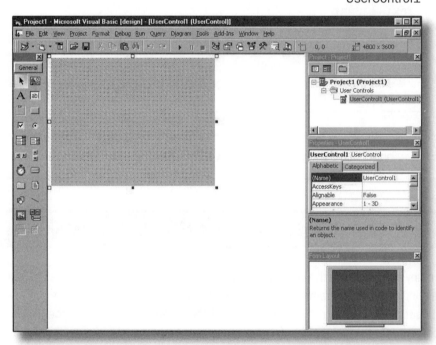

Before going any further you will make modifications to the UserControl1 properties and to the VB environment. First, scroll through the UserControl1 properties until you find the **ToolboxBitmap** property and then click on it. This property allows you to choose the icon that will represent your ActiveX control once it is added to the Toolbox. Click on the ellipse that appears. Select either the **Hand** or **Notebook** files in the Student Data & Resources files accompanying this course. Check with your instructor on the location of these files.

Once you have added the icon to the property, you will need to change some of the project properties. Open the Project menu and then click **Project Properties**. The Properties dialog box will appear as shown in Figure 9-11. Change the Project Name to **NewLabel**, and add the description shown in the Project Description text box. Then click **OK**.

You now need to add the *ActiveX Control Interface Wizard* from the Add-Ins menu. Click **Add-Ins** on the menu bar and then select **Add-In Manager**. The Add-In Manager dialog box shown in Figure 9-12 will open.

**FIGURE 9-11**
Project Properties dialog box

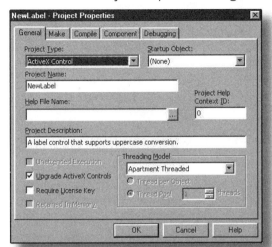

**FIGURE 9-12**
Add-In Manager dialog box

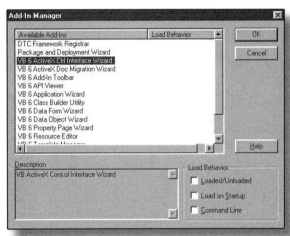

Double-click the **ActiveX Ctrl Interface Wizard** choice in the list box. The word *Loaded* will appear on the line next to the wizard's name. Then click the **OK** button, and the dialog box will close. Open the Add-Ins menu again, and you will see the ActiveX Control Interface Wizard displayed as an option below the Add-In Manager option.

You now have one more thing to do before you begin to create your ActiveX control. You need to add a regular Label control to UserControl1 before you can begin to modify it into your control.

Double-click the **Label** control in the Toolbox. The Label will appear in the middle of the user control with the caption "Label1." Rename the Label control to **lblParent**. You are now ready to use the wizard to create your ActiveX control.

### Step 3: ActiveX Control Interface Wizard

Everything is in place that you need to create your ActiveX control. Now it's time to run the wizard.

Open the Add-Ins menu, and then click the **ActiveX Control Interface Wizard** option. The first wizard dialog box opens as shown in Figure 9-13.

Click the **Next** button to move to the next screen. The next screen shown in Figure 9-14 will allow you to select the properties, events, and methods you would like to add to your control.

**FIGURE 9-13**
ActiveX Control Interface Wizard—Introduction

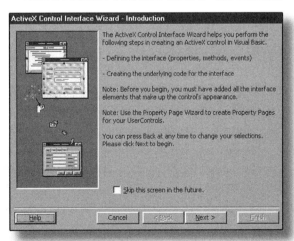

**197**

You select the properties, events, and methods you want to add from the left list box, and then click on the single, right-pointing arrow to add them to the controls in the right list box. By clicking on the double, right arrow you will add all the properties, events, and methods available to all controls. You do not want to do that. Select the following to add to your ActiveX control:

Alignment

Appearance

Caption

Change

All Font properties

ToolTipText

The most important property to be added is the Caption property because that is the one to be manipulated. Surprisingly, some of the preceding properties that you needed to add should be included by default, but they are not.

Once these are added, click the **Next** button. The next screen, shown in Figure 9-15, will allow you to add custom properties, events, or methods to your control.

For this project you will add one custom property. Click the **New** button, and the Add Custom Member dialog box will open as shown in Figure 9-16.

Type **UpperText** in the text box, leave the **Property** option button selected, and then click the **OK** button. Your new member will be added to the **My Custom Members** list box as shown in Figure 9-17.

Click the **Next** button to proceed to the next screen. The next screen, Set Mapping, will allow you to map your built-in properties, events, and methods to your control. You will map all members *except* for your custom UpperText property. Click on the first member in the text box, hold down the **Shift** key, scroll down the list box, and click on the next-to-last member. This will allow you to select all members except for your custom member, which will be the last one in the list. Figure 9-18 shows the Set Mapping screen after all the members have been selected. You will also need to choose **lblParent** from the Control drop-down list box. This choice will map all the members to your control.

**FIGURE 9-14**
ActiveX Control Interface Wizard—
Select Interface Members

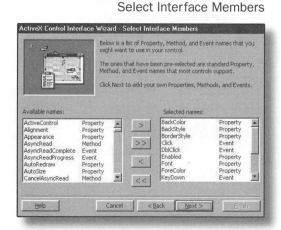

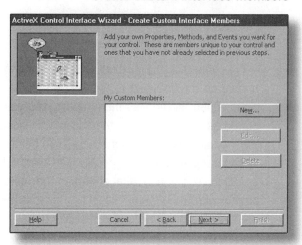

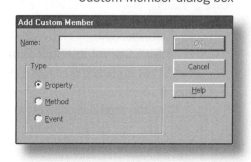

**198**

**FIGURE 9-17**
ActiveX Control Interface Wizard—
Create Custom Interface Members

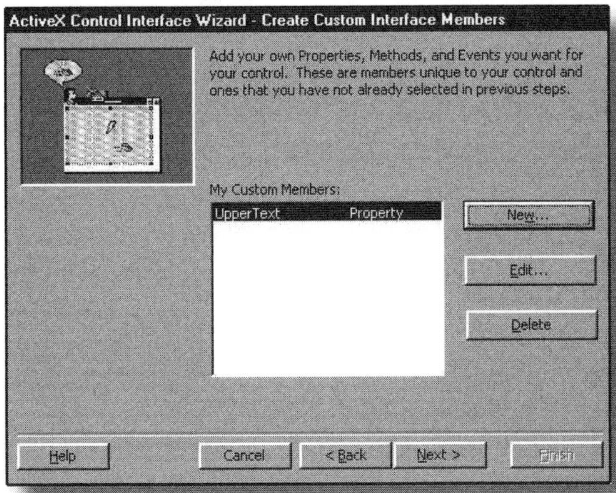

**FIGURE 9-18**
ActiveX Control Interface Wizard—
Set Mapping

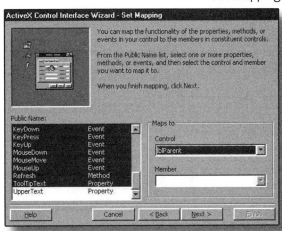

Click the **Next** button to proceed to the next screen. This screen, the Set Attributes screen, will allow you to modify the attributes of your custom member, if necessary. Click the **UpperText** member to highlight it. You will see its attributes as shown in Figure 9-19. Type the description shown in Figure 9-19 into the Description text box on your screen. The other attributes can be left as they are.

Click **Next** to proceed to the next screen. This is the last step of the ActiveX Control Interface Wizard. You will notice that the *View Summary Report* option is selected. This report will provide you with a summary of what is left to be done. If you would like to review this report, leave the check mark. If not, remove it. Click the **Finish** button to exit the wizard.

**FIGURE 9-19**
ActiveX Control Interface Wizard—Set Attributes

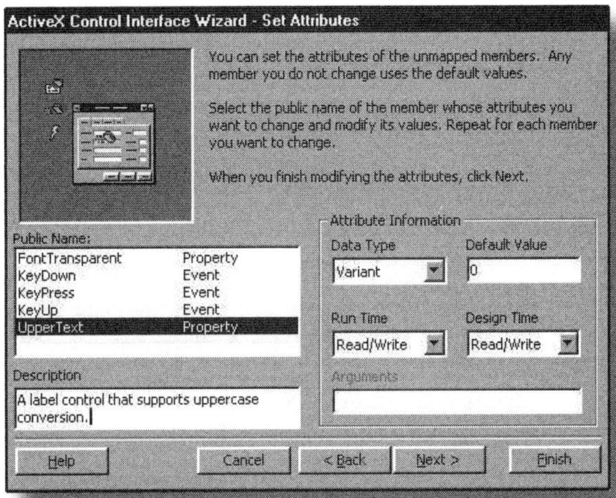

### Step 4: Add Code to Your Control

Your ActiveX control is almost finished. Before you can use it, you must make the property that you added fully functional. You will do this by adding and modifying a few parts of the code. Before you get to the code, you must realize that your ActiveX control, like all controls, comes with built-in functionality. In this project you will see the code that is attached to a typical label, and you will see your code. If some of the code is not understandable, do not worry about it. Understanding will come with experience.

Your UpperText property will be an *enumerated* property. When a user clicks on this property when using your label, he or she will get a choice of settings. In this case the settings will be *0* for NoChange or *1* for Uppercase. If the choice is 1, the label's caption will be in all capital letters. You need to define the enumerated values that will appear in the property.

Click **View** on the Menu bar, and then click the **Code** option. All the underlying code for your ActiveX control will be shown. The first lines of code you need to add will be added at the end of the General Declarations section of code. The block of code to be added is highlighted in Figure 9-20.

**FIGURE 9-20**
Enumerated property values code

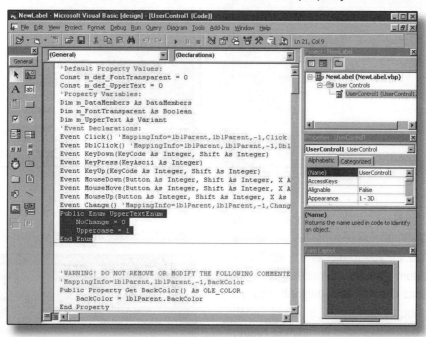

These two values will appear as value choices when the user decides to use your UpperText property. You now need to modify both the ***Get*** and ***Let procedures*** for your UpperText property. When a user accesses a property, the Get procedure is used. When the user sets a property value, the Let procedure is used. Both the Get and Let procedures should be stored together at the bottom of the code list. The reason is that all the procedures are in alphabetical order based on their related property names. So scroll down toward the bottom of the code list until you find the Get procedure for UpperText. The Let procedure will immediately follow the Get procedure. Modify the code as shown in Figure 9-21. Do *not* modify any of the comments or any other sections of the code! Modifications will cause your control to function improperly.

You are now ready to implement your control. But first you need to save your project. Your project is the design of the control. In order to implement the control, you must compile and save it on your system.

**FIGURE 9-21**

UpperText Get and Let procedure code

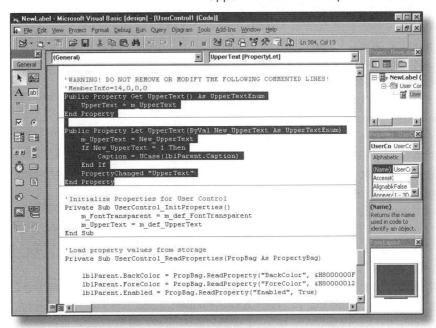

## Step 5: Save Your Project

Save your project changes by clicking on the **Save** button on the toolbar. Save the new UserControl as **UserControl1** and the project as **NewLabel**. The control will be saved with a **.ctl** extension, and the project will have the typical **.vbp** extension. The reason you are saving the project as *NewLabel* is that this is what your project does—it creates a new label. You will test your new control in Project 9-3.

## Step 6: Compile Your Control

**FIGURE 9-22**

Make Project dialog box

All ActiveX controls must be compiled before they can be used. You will now compile your control. Click **File** on the Menu bar, and then click the **Make NewLabel.ocx** option. The Make Project dialog box appears as shown in Figure 9-22. Choose the correct folder in which to save your control and name it **NewLabel**. Then click **OK**. If there are no errors, your control will compile in the folder you have chosen.

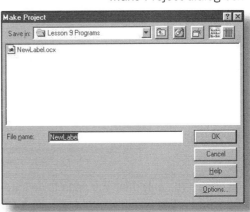

If you encounter any errors, the most likely cause is that you included properties, events, or methods that do not normally belong to a label. Simply "comment-out" the offending blocks of code and recompile. That will solve your most common problem. If you followed these steps exactly, you should not experience even that minor problem.

Now that your control has compiled, you can put it to use!

## Step 7: Create Project 9-3

This project will be very simple because its sole purpose will be to test your control. Create a new project. Name the project **Project9_3** and the form **frm9_3**. Before proceeding you will need to add your ActiveX control to the Toolbox.

Click **Projects** on the Menu bar, and then select the **Components** option. The Components dialog box will open, and all the ActiveX controls on your system will appear in the list box as shown in Figure 9-23. Your ActiveX control should be at the top of the list. If not, simply search for your description, "A label control that supports uppercase conversion." Place a check mark in your control's check box and then click **OK**. Your control's icon, either the Hand or the Notebook, will appear in the Toolbox.

**FIGURE 9-23**
Components dialog box

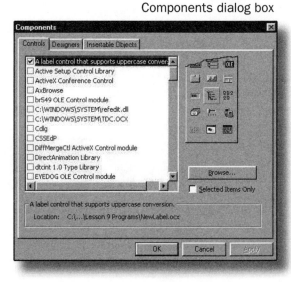

To place your control on your form, click on the control, and then draw it on the form. Make your control large enough so that you can see the caption "Label1" as shown in Figure 9-24. You can also change the form caption to read as shown in Figure 9-24.

**FIGURE 9-24**
Project 9-3 control layout

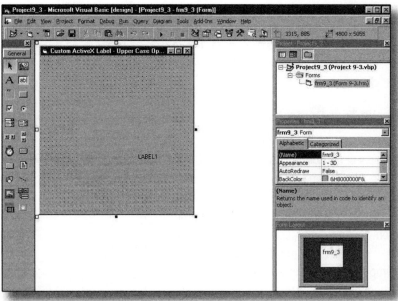

The only thing you need to do to test your control is to select the **UpperText** property from the Properties window and select the **1-Uppercase** option. Your Label1 caption should change to all uppercase. You now have a working ActiveX control that you created.

## Step 8: Save Your Project

Save your project by clicking the **Save** button on the toolbar. Save the form as **Form 9-3** and the project as **Project 9-3**.

**202**

### Step 9: Review Your Code

Now that your program has run successfully, answer the following questions. Review your answers with your classmates and teacher.

**1.** Explain the following block of code:

```
Public Enum UpperTextEnum
    NoChange = 0
    Uppercase = 1
End Enum
```

_____

_____

**2.** Explain the following block of code:

```
Public Property Get UpperText() As UpperTextEnum
    UpperText = m_UpperText
End Property
```

_____

_____

_____

**3.** Explain the following block of code:

```
Public Property Let UpperText(ByVal New_UpperText As UpperTextEnum)
    m_UpperText = New_UpperText
    If New_UpperText = 1 Then
        Caption = UCase(lblParent.Caption)
    End If
    PropertyChanged "UpperText"
End Property
```

_____

_____

_____

_____

# *Summary*

This lesson focused on ActiveX. ActiveX controls are an outgrowth of VB control extensions that became so popular that Microsoft was forced to rewrite them so that they would work with multiple products. ActiveX controls are now created and sold by various companies, so programmers have a vast selection of programming tools from which to choose.

You used the Microsoft Multimedia Control in an application. You created a wave file player with this control that allows you to play the wave sound files that come with Windows and other products.

Then you were introduced to ActiveX automation, which allows you to interact with another application from within your application. Instead of rewriting the functionality of an existing program into your program, you can simply borrow what you need. The only requirement is that the program be listed in your registry as having ActiveX automation.

**203**

The last part of this lesson dealt with creating your own ActiveX control. Of the three methods mentioned, you were introduced to the simplest. Remember that ActiveX is complex and will take time to master. You now have the ability to use, automate, and create ActiveX controls. Keep practicing and expand your abilities!

## LESSON 9 REVIEW QUESTIONS

### SHORT ANSWER

**Define the following in the space provided.**

1. ActiveX

   _____

   _____

2. ActiveX automation

   _____

   _____

3. Automation language

   _____

4. Components dialog box

   _____

5. Registry

   _____

   _____

6. Class

   _____

   _____

7. Subclass

   _____

8. Inheritance

   _____

   _____

9. Microsoft Multimedia Control

   _____

   _____

10. ActiveX Control Interface Wizard

   _____

   _____

**11.** Enumerated property

_____

## WRITTEN QUESTIONS

**Write your answers to the following questions in the space provided.**

**1.** Explain the relationship between ActiveX, OLE, COM, and DCOM.

_____
_____
_____
_____
_____

**2.** Provide an example of ActiveX automation.

_____
_____

**3.** Explain three ways of creating ActiveX controls.

_____
_____
_____
_____
_____

**4.** Explain the process of creating an ActiveX control by use of a simple subclass.

_____
_____
_____
_____
_____

**5.** Explain inheritance.

_____
_____
_____

**6.** Explain the Get and Let procedures used in your ActiveX control code.

_____
_____
_____

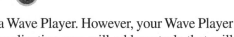

**Estimated Time:**

Application 9-1  2 ¹/₂ hours
Application 9-2  1 ¹/₂ hours

### APPLICATION 9-1

In Project 9-1 you used an existing ActiveX control to create a Wave Player. However, your Wave Player simply shows the MMC; it offers no other information. In this application you will add controls that will show the name of the wave file being played and the status of the player (which buttons are being clicked).

1.  Open your **Project 9-1**. Save your form as **SimpleWave2**, and then save your project as **App9-1**.

2.  Add four labels to your form. The first two labels will identify the information that will be displayed in the last two labels.

3.  The first set of labels will identify the wave file being played. The second set of labels will identify the status of the MMC.

4.  Add code to the StatusUpdate() event procedure that will display the wave file name being played and the status of the MMC. This is a built-in procedure that comes with your MMC.

5.  Save your project.

6.  Run your project to test it. Then debug it if necessary. Run it again.

### APPLICATION 9-2

In Project 9-3 you created your own ActiveX control—a modification of the Label control. In this application you will create an application that shows the difference and the benefit of converting captions to uppercase using a normal label control and your ActiveX label control.

1.  Create a new project with one form. Save the form as **Form App9-2** and the project as **App9-2**.

2.  Design your form to include one normal label, your ActiveX label, and one command button. Remember that you must add your control to the Toolbox before using it.

3.  Use any text you choose for the Caption value of both labels. You may need to make your label control slightly larger to see the caption.

4.  The command button code will cause both label control captions to convert to all capital letters. When you code your ActiveX control, you will notice that VB helps you find the properties that you want to use by providing a drop-down list of choices, just like it does with all the other controls. You will also be provided with choices for your custom property.

5.  Save your project.

6.  Run your project to test it. Then debug it if necessary. Run it again.

## CRITICAL THINKING

**Estimated Time: 5 hours**

1.  Using Project 9-2, which used ActiveX automation to create a spreadsheet, modify the program to accept more than one row of values into the spreadsheet before saving the file.

2.  Modify your NewLabel project to correct the size problem with your ActiveX control.

# PORTING APPLICATIONS TO THE INTERNET

LESSON

10

## *Introduction*

$V$isual Basic is one of the easiest programming languages to use for Internet access. However, this does not eliminate the need for you to become familiar with the more common Internet tools and languages. *Java*, *HTML*, *DHTML*, and *VBScript* are the main languages with which to begin gaining experience.

Visual Basic features the *Visual Basic Application Wizard*, which is used to develop applications that access the Internet. That type of access is important in some applications; however, with your ability to design your own applications, adding this functionality is simple and is something you can explore on your own. You will concentrate on *porting applications* to the Internet in this lesson.

Porting applications is a method by which your existing applications can be converted into *Internet-ready applications*. You will add the *ActiveX Document Migration Wizard* to your Add-Ins menu and then use the wizard to migrate one of your applications into an *ActiveX document*. An ActiveX document is simply an ActiveX control that has been migrated from a VB application. Each form in an application becomes an ActiveX document. If you have a single form application, you get one ActiveX document. Multiple forms each become separate ActiveX documents. Each form, therefore, is actually its own control. By compiling each ActiveX document-based application, you can run them within your browser without running VB.

You will port your applications without writing any HTML. The browser itself will execute the application, and if you place your application on a Web server, users anywhere in the world can access it (as long as their browser is ActiveX-compatible). What this means is that everything you have written in VB can be directly published to the Internet. But keep in mind that you are only scratching the surface in dealing with Internet applications. If your goals include programming for the Internet, you will definitely need to expand your abilities by studying other tools and languages.

This lesson focuses on the following:

■ **Explaining how to port applications to the Internet.** You will be able to explain how to use the ActiveX Document Migration Wizard to port applications to the Internet.

■ **Using the ActiveX Document Migration Wizard to create your own ActiveX document-based application.** You will migrate one of your existing applications into an ActiveX document and then port it to the Internet using the wizard.

## PROJECT 10-1:
## ActiveX Document Migration Wizard

Ⓑ

You will add the ActiveX Document Migration Wizard to your Add-Ins and then use it in this project. This wizard allows you to port your VB applications to the Internet.

You will create a compiled ActiveX document-based application from one of your earlier projects. Anyone with an ActiveX-compatible browser will be able to access your document if you place it on a Web server. You will be able to use these same steps to port any of your applications to the Internet.

### Step 1: Start Your Compiler

Start your compiler if it is not already running.

### Step 2: Add the ActiveX Document Migration Wizard

Open the Add-Ins menu and then click the **Add-In Manager**. The Add-In Manager dialog box will open. Double-click the **ActiveX Doc Migration Wizard** as shown in Figure 10-1. The word "Loaded" will appear on the same line. Click the **OK** button to close the dialog box. The wizard is now loaded on your Add-Ins menu.

### Step 3: Open Project 1-1

Open the **File** menu and click **Open Project**. The Existing tab should be displayed in the Open Project dialog box. Open your **Project 1-1** project file. The project will look like Figure 10-2. Run your application to make sure it works as it did when you created it. Then stop your application.

**FIGURE 10-1**
Add-In Manager dialog box

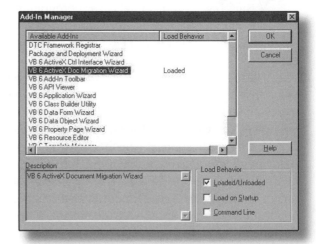

**FIGURE 10-2**
Project 1-1

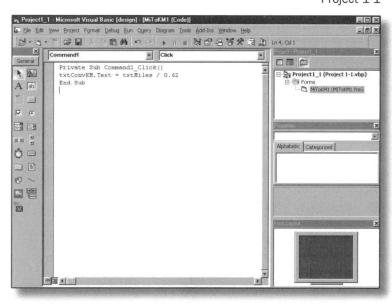

## Step 4: Start the Migration Wizard

Open the Add-Ins menu and then click the **ActiveX Document Migration Wizard** option. The first wizard dialog box opens as shown in Figure 10-3. Click **Next** to continue.

The next window that opens is the Form Selection window as shown in Figure 10-4. In this window you will select the form that you are migrating. Because Project 1-1 has only the **MiToKM1** form, that is the one you will select. Click the **Next** button.

**FIGURE 10-3**
ActiveX Document Migration
Wizard—Introduction

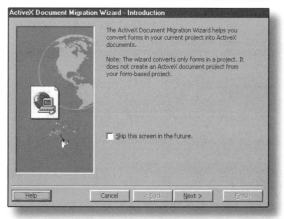

**FIGURE 10-4**
ActiveX Document Migration
Wizard—Form Selection

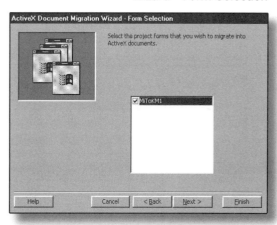

The next window is the Options window as shown in Figure 10-5. The options referred to are those you would like performed if VB encounters invalid code and the type project to which you would like yours converted. Your project should have no invalid code, but if it did, commenting it out would keep the problem code but allow you the opportunity to correct it. You may also want to consider removing the forms that are converted because those forms will now reside in an ActiveX document. Try it both ways later in order to compare the differences.

You want to convert your project to an **ActiveX EXE**, so leave that choice selected. Click the **Next** button.

The last wizard dialog box appears, as shown in Figure 10-6. Make sure **Yes** is selected so that you will see a Summary Report, which will provide you with details of what still needs to be done. Click the **Finish** button.

**FIGURE 10-5**
ActiveX Document Migration Wizard—Options

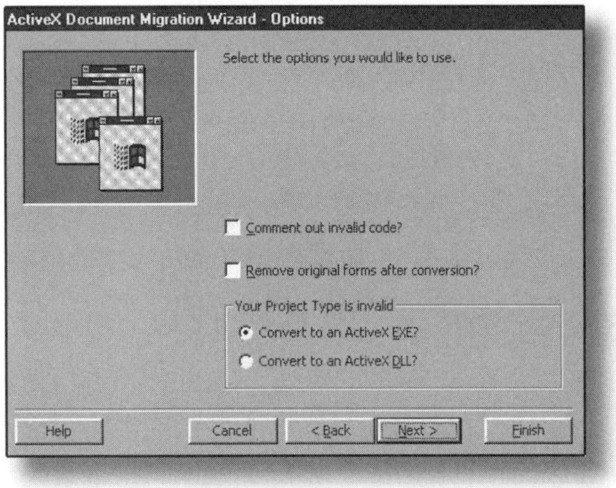

**FIGURE 10-6**
ActiveX Document Migration Wizard—Finished

A message box will appear as shown in Figure 10-7, stating that your ActiveX document was created. Click **OK** to continue.

If you chose to view the Summary Report, the report will be displayed on your screen as shown in Figure 10-8. Either close the report or save it by clicking the appropriate button.

**FIGURE 10-7**
ActiveX Document(s) Created

**FIGURE 10-8**
ActiveX Document Migration Wizard Summary Report

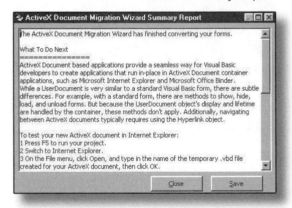

Notice that your project now contains a **User Document** named *docMiToKM1.dob*. This document is highlighted in Figure 10-9. Now that you are finished with the wizard, you must run your application once more to prepare an executable ActiveX document object.

**210**

**FIGURE 10-9**

User Document—docMiToKM1.dob

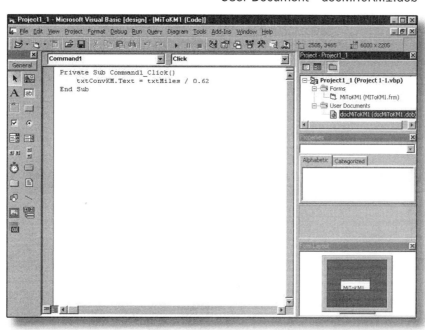

## Step 5: Preparing the Executable ActiveX Document

Click the **Run** button on the VB toolbar. Your application will begin to execute. The Project1_1 Project Properties dialog box will open as shown in Figure 10-10.

The **Start component** is the ActiveX document you created when you executed your program. Click **OK** to start the ActiveX document. This document will start within your Internet browser. Figure 10-11 shows the ActiveX document running within Microsoft's Internet Explorer 4.0. Test your ActiveX document by entering figures and clicking the command button. Then close your Internet browser.

> ### HOT TIP
>
> If you are creating your ActiveX document with Visual Basic 5.0, skip Step 5 and proceed to Step 6.

**FIGURE 10-10**

Project1_1 Project Properties dialog box

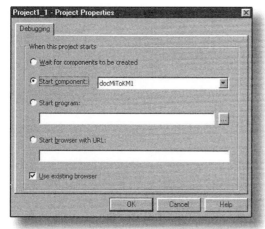

**FIGURE 10-11**

docMiToKM1 within Internet Explorer 4.0

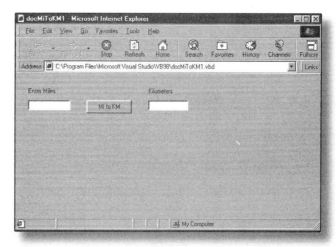

You now need to create a compiled ActiveX document-based application from this project.

## Step 6: Compiling the ActiveX Document-Based Application

In order to compile your project into an ActiveX document-based application, you must add your User Document to an Activex Document Exe file. First, close your open project and then start a new project. When the New Project dialog box opens, double-click the **Activex Document Exe** icon.

**FIGURE 10-12**
Activex Document Exe project

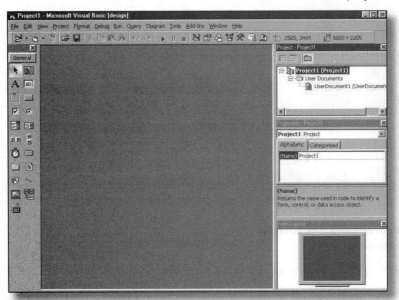

A new project opens with no form as shown in Figure 10-12. The only object that this project contains is a default User Document as shown in the Project window.

You need to add the User Control from your modified Project 1-1 to this project. Click **Project** on the Menu bar and then select the **Add User Document** option. When the Add User Document dialog box opens, find your **docMiToKM1.dob** file, as shown in Figure 10-13, and then click **Open**. Your User Document is added to the project.

Before moving on, you need to remove the default user document from the project. Highlight **UserDocument1** in the Project window. Open the **Project** menu and then select **Remove UserDocument1**.

The last step before compiling is to rename your project. Name your project **Project10_1**.

**FIGURE 10-13**
Add User Document—docMiToKM1.dob

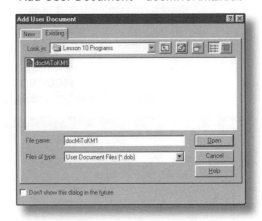

## Step 7: Make Project10_1.exe

You now need to make your compiled ActiveX document-based application. Open the **File** menu and select **Make Project10_1.exe**, as shown in Figure 10-14.

The Make Project dialog box opens. Find the proper folder in which to save your compiled project and then click **OK**. Your project will compile and then save to the chosen folder.

**FIGURE 10-14**
Make Project10_1.exe

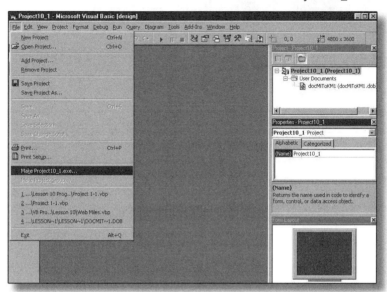

### Step 8: Test Your Project

Test the project by opening your ActiveX-compatible Internet browser. When your browser opens, click **File** on the Menu bar and then select **Open**. Browse to the folder in which you compiled your ActiveX document. Select the file **docMiToKM1.vbd**, and then click **OK**. If you do not see your file in the folder, change the file type from HTML to **All Files**. Also, if you use Internet Explorer 4.0, the icon for this file will be an IE icon.

When you click **OK**, another instance of your browser will open, executing your ActiveX document. If you place your ActiveX document on a Web server, anyone with an ActiveX compatible Internet browser will be able to execute it.

You can use the preceding process to port any of your other applications to the Internet! And you wrote no HTML to produce the Web page.

 **HOT TIP**

You may encounter problems running your ActiveX document with Netscape Navigator. With the differences between Internet Explorer and Netscape Navigator, this is not surprising. Simply test your document with Internet Explorer.

# *Summary*

You ported one of your applications to the Internet in this lesson without having to write HTML code. You can use the same process with your other applications.

You added the ActiveX Document Migration Wizard to your VB environment and used this wizard to create an ActiveX document from an existing project form that will run within an ActiveX-compatible browser. In order to allow the ActiveX document to run without VB being started, you compiled your ActiveX document. You added your User Document to an ActiveX Document.exe project and then compiled it in order to meet the necessary requirements.

Even though this process is easy, remember that it does not replace the other tools and programming languages needed to develop great Web pages. You still need to gain experience with Java, HTML, DHTML, VBScript, and other tools in order to develop your Web design abilities.

You now have the ability to port your applications to the Internet. Keep developing your Internet abilities!

## LESSON 10 REVIEW QUESTIONS

### SHORT ANSWER

**Define the following in the space provided.**

1. Java

2. HTML

3. DHTML

4. VBScript

5. Visual Basic Application Wizard

6. Porting applications

7. Internet-ready application

8. ActiveX Document Migration Wizard

9. ActiveX document

10. User document

11. ActiveX-compatible Internet browser

## CRITICAL THINKING

 **Estimated Time: 6 hours**

1. Using the process described in this lesson, port another of your projects to the Internet.

2. Using the process described in this lesson, port a multiform project to the Internet.

# INDEX